# My Wia

## Mike Pratt

*Including drawings – the drawings in the text are the author's sketches drawn in the field and taken straight from his notebooks along the way.*

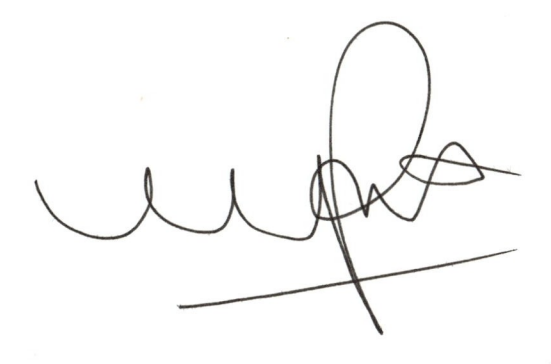

Red Squirrel Press

First published in the UK in 2015 by
Red Squirrel Press
Briery Hill Cottage
Stannington
Morpeth
NE61 6ES
www.redsquirrelpress.com

Second Edition printed 2016

Red Squirrel Press is distributed by Central Books Ltd and represented by Inpress. Ltd.
www.inpressbooks.co.uk

Edited by Pauline Plummer

Cover image 'Blawearie' by © Darryn Wade

Copyright © Mike Pratt 2015

The right of Mike Pratt to be identified as the author of this work has been asserted by him in accordance with Section 77 of the Copyright, Designs and Patents Act 1988. All rights reserved.
A CIP catalogue record is available from the British Library.

ISBN: 978 1 910437 20 9

Printed by Charlesworth Press.

# Contents

**My Wild Northumbria**
**Border-Lands, to the Start of it all...**     **9**
Mountain Top     11
Aromatic Eildons     15
Old Oakey     20
The Street     25
Cheviot Machismo     29
**Northumbria-Land, to the Heart of it all...**     **34**
Pilgrim's Crossing     36
Blawearie     40
Red Squirrel Country     45
A Skyspace     50
Wall     54
Look Outs     58
Druridge     62
Looks Could Kill     65
Geo-Logic     68
Water and Witches     73
Magpie Architecture     77
A Pet Corncrake!     81
**Bishop-Land, to the Heads of it all...**     **86**
Meadowlands     87
Tupperware Frogs     93
Red Kite Overhead     95
Famous Grouse     99
Marilyns     103

| | |
|---|---|
| **Yorkshire-Lands, to the Guts of it all…** | **108** |
| Merlin Moors | 110 |
| Flyover | 118 |
| Rough Legged Sleddale | 122 |
| Quarry Owls | 126 |
| To the Wainstones | 131 |
| Our Beach | 137 |
| Seymour and other hawks | 140 |
| Alpine Mulgrave | 144 |
| Agar's Gap | 149 |
| Down Kettleness | 151 |
| Bears and Wolves | 155 |
| Whales' Bones | 158 |
| **Humber-Wold Land, to the wet Feet of it all…** | **163** |
| Nature's Apprentice | 164 |
| Marshlands | 169 |
| Spurned at Spurn | 174 |
| The YOC | 178 |
| Boxers | 182 |
| Eden | 186 |
| **Edge-Lands, to the Ends of it all…** | **192** |
| The Falls | 194 |
| The Bowland Harriers | 199 |
| Skelghyll | 204 |
| Merseysiders | 207 |
| The Hen Cloud | 211 |
| Postscript | 216 |
| Selected Further Reading | 217 |
| Acknowledgements and Thanks | 219 |

*For Mam, who helped me with my 'composition' and sports editorship of the Errington Monthly, and Dad who first showed me a Sledmere chaffinch.*

My 'Mindmap' of Northumbria

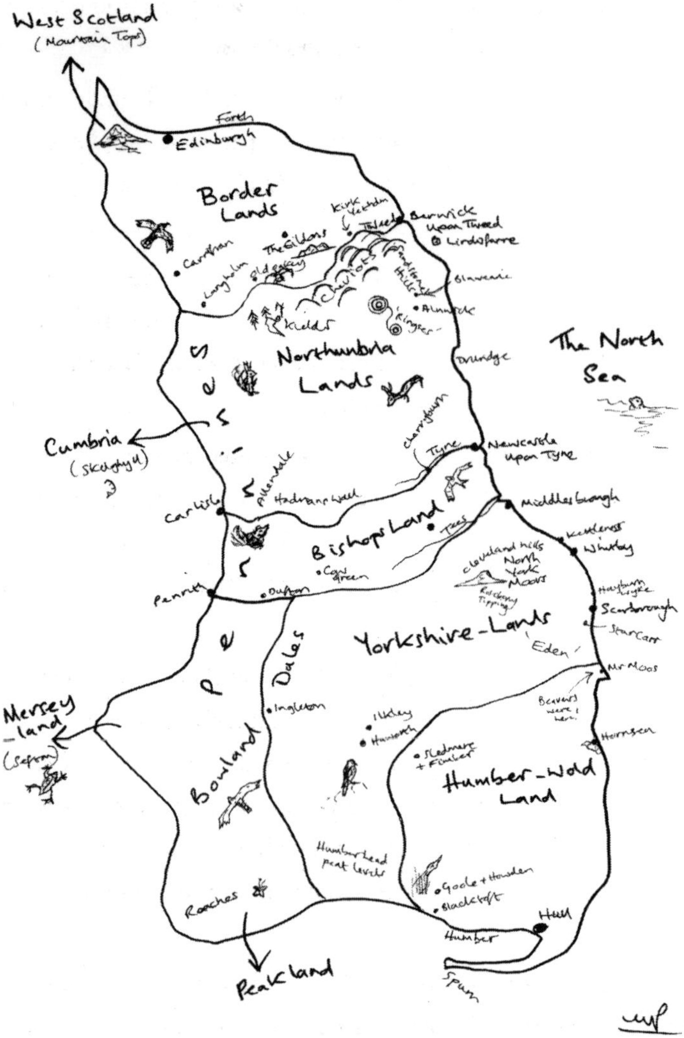

# *My Wild Northumbria*

My Wild Northumbria tracks the geography of my life in the North East of England, an exploration and experience of its landscapes and wildlife and their relationship with people over decades.

In the last four years I have revisited the familiar, dug into memories and discovered new places to complete a personal 'mind map' of the region, which roughly equates to the old Kingdom of Northumbria, at its greatest 7th Century extent.

This ranged from Edinburgh and the Scottish Borders in the north, to the Humber in the south and inland to the Pennines, venturing briefly into Lancashire, Cumbria and the Peak District. It is my eastern-centric view of 'the North'.

Along the way I have been constantly inspired by the prehistoric and historic and human spiritual perspectives that form an intrinsic part of the North East's sense of place. These, in turn, have influenced how we live here, always close to Nature, if we choose to recognise it or seek it out.

The Celtic Christian traditions of Saint Cuthbert and others are still palpable here, the first naturalists of Northumbria, who felt spiritually connected to Nature, through their open air, wandering pilgrimages. That they followed in the footsteps of earlier people, who felt this and expressed it in different ways is obvious too; it is carved and written in the stones and land everywhere. I am following in their footsteps.

My focus is always the 'wild' and 'natural', though these are relative terms, qualities you find in yourself, as much as outdoors. I mean a sense of place where naturalness prevails and where there is a presence of landscape, countryside and living creatures.

This journey then has taken me from the raw, remote hills of Northumberland and The Borders, to familiar and unfamiliar parts of Yorkshire and Humberside, from sea and coast to fell and fen, to bog and wood, to the surviving and temporary green bits in cities and towns and most elements of what make up the natural living history of old and new Northumbria.

The essays try to capture the essence of places and wild creatures in their local settings and put them in a wider connected context. They mark the contrasts in landscape along the way and the focus on places and species that are important and meaningful to me, I feel part of this naturalness, however encountered.

Someone else, you, would surely have picked different places, species and had different experiences, or not even recognised the cohesiveness I feel and see here in the greater North East of England but this is my take on things; it is My Wild Northumbria.

*To the Start of it all,*
*wild adventures in the Scottish Borders*

# Border-Lands

This is in-between land, the threshold between two countries, which for centuries, even today, has been wrestled over. The landscape sets it apart at once, sets the scene for its reputation as being slightly ungovernable: a place to disappear into.

Sparsely populated, conical mountains and rolling, steep, hill country made it the ideal place for the 'mosstrooper' reivers, the cattle rustlers, folk heroes and horse thieves who lived here from medieval times. They alone could navigate the wilderness of mosses and bogs, moor and flushes and sharp hills that made up most of the country then, as now. It has always been a place for outsiders, where the Gypsy Queen was crowned and Kings and Queens of many clans escaped to hide out.

Today there remains a sense of this past. The views of endless hills from Kielder Moor or the Milfield Plain, give the impression of a vast, unpopulated, wild country, largely untouched. It is a place where the golden eagle and raven still soar, and from which the pine marten slinks south, the latest of many to foray into the edge of England.

It is a connecting place too. It was through these borderlands that the Celtic monks travelled from the west of Ireland and Scotland, to set up their Lindisfarne monastery, the Iona, or 'Holy Isle', of the east. It is where the old Kingdom started, waxed and waned. Long before this, the east-west axis existed as a cultural and trade route, the first farmers and perhaps hunter gatherers, before them, extending kinship through the hill country. You can still follow their paths, etched into the hillsides and valleys.

There is always something challenging and a little mysterious about the border hills and moors. Untamed Nature is a possibility here, an uncompromising landscape that belongs to no one.

*(Unidentified mountain, somewhere west of Edinburgh)*

# Mountain Top

It all started when, on a whim, I climbed a mountain.

Irresponsible, stupid, should know better, said one part of me; spontaneous, adventurous, said another. My heart led me where my head said no, unprepared, up a proper mountain, strangely drawn, compelled upwards at speed.

Straight up the conical, classically shaped mountains back I paced, no water, food, little gear, except good boots and a hat, a thin jumper.

It was late afternoon, the sun coming to an end as I started off. It was mild at ground level but conditions changed for the worse as I rose. The path was good but steep and rocky, a well laid track leading me up, horizon by horizon.

I just wanted to climb it, there and then. I felt I could. There was no choice. I simply had to.

I went up, the temperature went down; I speeded up to keep warm. Lungs heaved, legs shook with the effort, and I breathed deeply and moved on, climbing all the time, never resting for long, rising into the sky.

It was exhilarating. I was high on the adrenalin of the risk and the mental focus, pure exertion, the immediacy of it all. I knew it was not a good idea to go this far up, with no provisions so late in the day and with no one knowing where I was. I passed only three people, coming down.

But I had seen this peak in the distance as I drove about exploring, picked it out of the landscape, or it picked me.

I climbed higher, the cloud got lower. The landscape was revealed and hidden by turns, as the scheming clouds lifted and fell.

It was ravishing all around me, endless and wild, untamed high-lands, Munro, after Munro, disappearing into the distance, some still snow topped, even in June. It felt like the whole of the distant Scottish Borders and beyond was within my view and grasp, if only I could keep climbing.

I reached the first summit at last. There's always more than one, isn't there? This was very much a false one, a mere shoulder to lie on and gaze up to the crown, still way above, on a sharpening ridge, with much to do in between to get there. The real endeavour was just about to begin.

But no matter that this should have been it, that what I had been making for had almost been attained, that the temperature was now 'fit to cut you in two', the wind chill getting nasty, I would not be beaten back. The symbolism of only getting so far up the mountain was too much; I pressed on.

The well-made path stopped there though, abruptly. Instead, a massive boulder field of angled igneous blocks guarded the summit. A thin path of sorts, of mountain goats perhaps, veered off along the precipitous edge. I was forced to turn in and up, to hop from rock to block, to make progress.

My energy was running out. Legs heavy, head racing, low blood sugar kicked in, a deep hunger, and a hollowness crept upon me like a slow ache. I pushed myself, made my legs climb, sucking in and tightening my stomach muscles to help. It was further than I imagined, than it had looked. The view was now a background to a growing sense of inner desperation.

I took shelter thirty metres from the top, under a big stone, cowering from the wind and cold, panting and shaking. I had to admit to being scared. If it rained now I would end up with exposure. I could feel my internal system shutting down, a slight feeling of delirium.

Despite the jaw-stretching, inner tiredness I still had some power in me and a determination, however misguided. I would get to the top, make a break for it then get back down as quick as I could. Hanging about and savouring the experience was not an option. I needed sustenance, warmth, retreat.

I went for it, bolting out of my cavity, facing the wind straight in the chest. Rock, by massive rock, I made it, to the very peak. I pivoted there on the highest jutting point a few moments, head literally in the clouds. I was startled by my own actions, the mix of emotions, elation, bemusement, and a sudden rush of 'bliss'. I really wasn't sure I was going to make it back, but, at that point, I did not care.

So many mountaineers and hill walkers must feel this way, overcome by the moment and effort and I realised that this was a major part of why I was here and why they risk themselves too; this sense of joy and danger is a heady mix. I had somehow gone beyond myself and part of me could have, wanted to, take an additional step into nothingness.

But it was the thirst that got me back to my senses and the gnawing hunger again. I thought of the old, soft packet of biscuits I'd left in the car boot, the abandoned toffee under the seat. I leapt down and jostled, skipped, jogged as best I could back down the boulder field.

Even in this state the stark beauty and drama of the setting did not escape me, far from it. This was part of the whole rush, the edge was the inhospitableness of it all. Nature, I realised, was indifferent, I mattered little, yet I felt totally alive. I was there, just feeling, part of the whole.

My descent was frantic, staccato, shock absorbing. Everything was shaking by now, my breath, body and confidence. But I knew I could do it once I was below the boulders and back on the main track, despite its steepness and length; about two hours downhill still to go, if only I wasn't about to collapse with hunger and cold.

But I picked up. The lower I got, the faster I walked, ran even. Ran into the open arms of the soft foothill underbelly of this great mountain, ran past the trees and little gathering streams, ran into the welcome relief and protection of the car park, my car there waiting.

Doors were flung open. Rolling on the back seat, diving under it for that toffee, there were three! I chewed them all down like a dog, raided the boot for the old biscuits and water I kept for the radiator.

I shouldn't have done it. It was irresponsible and reckless. I had thrilled myself with the achievement and experience, above all the freedom it brought. But that wasn't, in itself, enough to justify courting danger for myself and perhaps others, who might have had to find or rescue me. I knew that rationally.

Despite this something underneath made it acceptable, by-passing the guilt. It was all about the fear. That fearlessness on the ascent and the fearfulness on the descent; the pure fear on the summit and that moment when I might have stepped off.

There was a transcendence on this mountain, above and beyond my survival instincts, something I couldn't have achieved if I'd been planned and prepared. I had needed to feel unsafe.

Spiritually and physically I had travelled to 'the top of the mountain'. In so doing I had kindled in myself an appetite for a journey of wild discovery that would take me, over months, from one end of the old Kingdom of Northumbria, to the other, in search again of natural elation.

*(The Eildon Hills,*
*Melrose, Kelso)*

## Aromatic Eildons

Red is the colour of the Eildon Hills, red of stone and soil. Today I follow in the footsteps of a red fox, who scent marked the trail, while I was having breakfast.

Its musky odour stays just in front of me, from Melrose Abbey to Newstead and I even pick it up again, as I start to scale the side of the first of the three pointed hills. As if to emphasise its presence, the fox's territorial scats mark my upward progress, as regularly placed as the official way-markers.

It gives me a fox nosed impression of The Borders, its undulating farmland rising from the Tweed, until it forms the distinctive Eildons, tripartite cones. I feel the fox is marking me as I climb, hiding in the woods or bracken, so that I half expect a glimpse of my foxy companion around each corner.

It put me in mind of a similar occasion, where I tracked a mile along the River Rye, in the snow, the blood red trail of killed redwings, until finally a fox revealed itself, scarlet against the snow, on the bank ahead, gorging on its latest victim.

This is a place of surprises and high expectation. These hills stand out for miles around and have attracted attention from prehistory, mythology being woven around their morphology. But, as I discover repeatedly throughout my journey, you create your own story from your direct experience of landscape and place, picking up on the landscape cues that appeal uniquely to you.

Today it is the conspiring of weather and sense of smell that frame my experience of the Eildons.

You can't help but be influenced by their folklore and histories. The Eildon's natural assets have accumulated symbolic meaning. Their three peaks lent themselves to the ancient worship of the three Celtic goddesses, also taken up by the Romans, who made their Tritontium camp nearby. Bronze and Iron Age peoples made encampments and a festival site on the North Hill plateau and the springs flowing out of them were venerated from prehistoric to Christian times.

Most intriguing of all is the legend that the lands around the Eildons were a Fairy Kingdom. Thomas the Rhymer, a local craftsman, fell asleep under the once great Eildon tree and was awoken and charmed by the 'Queen of the Fairies', who stole him away for what felt like three days, but was in fact seven years. When she let him return to normality she had given him the gift and the curse of ever speaking the truth and for poetry and prophesy.

I come upon 'The Rhymer Stone' on my way up to the hills. It is an inscribed formal headstone that tells this story in fading letters, on the spot where once stood the famed tree. There is also a semi-circular platform and sculpted stone seat, inviting you to rest awhile and look out over the fields down to the river, to the edge of the Fairy Kingdom.

I do not spy any fairies on this occasion, though I do encounter a most beautiful daytime flying moth, a buff yellow graceful creature, rare enough of itself, on a damp late November morning. It would do today, for me, as a fairy, a bit of the super-natural encountered along the way.

Progressing uphill, I walk between double hedges of old coppice trees, including an impressive multi stemmed sallow; the land seems to paint me from head to foot, so that I become as red as the trail itself as I slide in the red mud. I stop to photograph a beautiful, moss-formed, old nest of a wren, its gaping entrance inviting the fingers and eyes of passers-by.

I had set out to get a step back view of the Cheviots and the Scottish-English border, as Saint Cuthbert would have seen them, while he was a young monk at Melrose Abbey, where he started his religious life. He would have crossed these hills at the start of his journey to Lindisfarne and beyond. More than anywhere else, this felt like the right place to properly start my Northumbrian journey.

I first spied them from the Cheviots. From there they had looked like a floating, three peaked island, on the far horizon.

Today is not a day for the views the Eildons are praised for. But as I scale the first, North Hill, I do get a buzzard's eye view of the undulating land, way into the distance, punctuated with other volcanic, cone-like protrusions, but the Cheviots stay lost in the mists.

The curtains close around me as I approach the flattish top of the hill. It is hard to imagine in the mizzle that this had been a site for sacred ceremony. You can just make out the remains of ditches and banks and flat hut platforms, but it is cold, damp and disorientating.

17

It is the minute details immediately around me I really notice, like the balls of light green lichen caught in the dry heather, bright red and yellow wax cap fungi, the contrast of the two lobed leaves of cloudberry, one leaf bright green, the other bright yellow. I pick up a wet and curled buzzard feather, brown and white, striped like a humbug. Having left old foxy behind, the smell now is of held-in moist soil and rock, the acidic burnt aroma of heather.

From the bracken I pick up a circle of twine-like heather and instinctively push it onto my right hand middle finger like a wooden ring, its old frond sweeping back over my hand, like some medieval filigree design. I wear it throughout the rest of the walk, as if, for a time, I am wedded to the hills.

My eyes are brought up again by the flight of grouse circling around the top of the hill, in the mists, as if they too are held in by the white out.

I don't linger, but spiral down to the saddle between the North Hill and Mid Hill, which should be called 'the Big Hill', as it is the tallest and steepest and slightly daunting now, as it towers upwards into thick cloud.

The way up is geological, exposed volcanic rocks and boulders poke out of the mist like big gargoyles and the path itself is a linear scree. Somehow I make good progress, though it is like walking with your eyes half shut. On top, the hill is totally wrapped around with cloud, though illuminated by some distant sun. It is like being in a white tent with a light outside. Serene, I lie on my back in the grass and close my eyes.

Then it's down again, sheer and fast, back to the saddle and curling around and along to the last of the summits, the Western Hill. I descend to the forest edge and around the foot of the big hill; at this level you can see and there are signs of the cloud lifting, a wind is getting up.

The top of the low rise of the Western Hill is not dramatic like the other two but forms a vantage point. As I get to the top there is a great reveal, the cloud is cast aside and bright sunlight floods the hills and landscape, right back to the outline of the Cheviots, seen clearly now. It is breath-taking and the hills are even more impressive for being so cloaked before.

Emboldened by the light, I run down to a fourth and lesser peak, the well named Little Hill, a relatively small cone with a cover of bright grass and a small crag. I am delighted to discover it is covered in waves of wild blewit mushrooms; I fill my hat and have the fruity aroma of these purple and brown mushrooms all the way back to Melrose.

I turn and follow a goat-like trail that circumnavigates the big hill and, as I do, spook a sparrohawk, chasing meadow pipits. The sun has brought all birdlife out; four ravens tumble and fall above the hill and I have a glimpse of a circling peregrine, warming its wings.

I follow the track of Saint Cuthbert's Way downhill, more red mud and fast flowing springs, noticing, among the boot prints of previous walkers, the little diamond shaped pads of a fox.

This half day walk, in all weathers, had seemed like a distillation of all the hills I'd ever encountered.

The final scents of the trail are not of fox or mushroom or damp soil and heather potpourri, but of rotting crab apples under a bush by a stile. They smell like old cider and make you thirst for their tart fruit.

Much more appetising is the 'oaty apple crumble' I consume afterwards in Russell's Restaurant, having first divested myself of the red boots and clothing I have acquired. I have started my quest now; I am on my way.

*(Outside Jedburgh, passing through, on the way to and from Scotland)*

## ***Old Oakey***

Like some great stilt walking creature from the abyss, caught in momentary stillness, the Capon Oak of Jedburgh stands supported in its old age, just off the A68, in the Scottish Borders.

Hidden behind hedges it is not at first obvious that this is one of the most historically significant veteran trees in the UK, in fact one of the top six trees in Scotland. It is a majestic tree of great age and character.

Trees like these have a power and charisma. This ten metre girth, old sessile oak, is so like the trees we imagine in fairy stories, gnarled and twisted, broken in two, its branches spreading in all directions, creating a low canopy of leaves and a yawning hollowness within; a hulk of a tree, still supporting hundreds of species of insect, bird and plants; an ecosystem all of its own.

Great muscular roots anchor it into the Earth; it is like a living sculpture, its long years, every twist and turn, manifested in its varied shapes and textures, soft and hard, rough and smooth, straight and bent, robust yet elegant. Like all veteran trees I have come across, I feel hushed in its presence. I need to touch it, feel its wrinkled bark and creviced limbs.

On this autumn visit, I notice something small and dark moving in the grass at its base. It is a toad, just going into hibernation, one of the many creatures that gain refuge in and around it. I pick it up briefly; the almost black, leathery skin emphasising its big golden eyes as it stares up at me indignantly.

I reflect on all the special trees I have encountered, over the years: ancient yews several thousand years old, in Welsh graveyards: the Major Oak in Sherwood, like this one, but even taller and more hollowed, more supported: grotesquely shaped, ancient ash trees in parks such as Belsay and at Howden: the Macbeth Oak, in Dunkeld that you can hide inside: another you could hold a small dinner party in: revered hollies and thorns next to springs and the massive old coppice limes, chestnuts and pollards of Iron Age and Roman descent. They are all portals to our wildwood past.

Yes, the Capon Oak has been around since Medieval times, is perhaps five hundred to a thousand years old, during which time it has seen borders and countries change and much besides: a silent witness to the changes in ourselves that have so affected all of Nature in turn, from thud of axe, to whir of chainsaw.

'Old Oakey' is a relic of the ancient Caledonian native forests, the great northern forest of Ettrick and Jedforest, that once covered

The Borders for miles, a largely natural forest of pine and oak, now reduced to nothing or modern day plantation forest.

Like all 'old dodders,' as Shakespeare called them, it is a national treasure, a monument to the past where we can absorb the passage of time it has lived through, against the odds, a rare survivor. Trees like this are catalysts of stories and inspiration, natural gathering places, foci of natural wisdom.

Having reached a stage of stasis, it is doddering into the final stages of its life. Even four hundred years ago, it was a place for the Capuchin monks of nearby Jedburgh Abbey to shelter beneath.

I stop every time I drive to and from Scotland to pay homage. The tree has something of the cathedral about it, a natural structure that invites our admiration and respect. When we stand under trees like the Capon Oak, their almost ageless presence makes us reflect on our comparably short lives and the significance, or otherwise, of all life. Old trees invite philosophy.

Across the world, people still use trees to meet and hold religious ceremonies beneath. They decorate them ceremonially with offerings, traditions as old as our evolution. In the UK we have lost a lot of the traditions of pagan and Celtic Christian tree worship and ceremony, but not entirely. They are still venerated and even new ceremonies are invented around significant trees. The Capon itself features in the annual July, Jethart Callant's Festival, where horsemen ride out and reclaim their lands, initiated in the 1940s.

I imagine The Capon Oak is lonely and hankers after a companion near its age and experience. Though there are trees nearby, they are mere saplings in comparison. I also guess she feels the absence of ancient forest that she was once part of, now long cut down and overgrazed.

But when I visit, I whisper into her hollow folds, stories of hope and optimism, about the efforts being made to rekindle the ancient forests across The Borders and if only she could uproot herself and go as far as Moffat to the north-west, she would be able to see some of the early results.

At Carrifran, a massive tree planting and regeneration project has been developed over the last fifteen years and a million trees have become established, ranging from alder, ash, cherry and elm in the valley bottom to hazel, holly, oak, and thorn, birch and alder on the crags, through to high montane willow and juniper scrub, growing once again, on the ridges of the steep old hills.

All of this has been accomplished by volunteers under the auspice of the Border Forest Trust and the Carrifran and John Muir Trusts. The pattern mimics those preserved as a record, in the peat and soils of the landscape of thousands of years ago, a primeval forest that stood here even long before the acorn that hatched the Capon Oak.

When I call in I can see how the trees are taking off, with good height trees now obvious in the valley and higher up. Some years back I ventured up here with a bad leg and regretted it as I tried, unsuccessfully, to keep up with the volunteer plantsmen, all retired and yet somehow mountain goat like in their ability to scale steep slopes to plant trees. Their enthusiasm and energy for their cause was unbounded. Another big hill nearby has been purchased and I have no doubt it too will be returned to a natural state of trees anytime soon, if they have anything to do with it.

These devoted restorers draw inspiration from the landscape and its history, from great old trees and woods that do survive. Also, I think, from a very lucky coincidence, or perhaps a symbolic event that got somehow chaotically programmed into the scheme of things to spur them on? We will never know.

This was the chance discovery, just before planting was started in 1990, of a 6000 year old hunter's yew bow in the bog at Rotten Bottom, on the plateau at the head of Carrifran Valley. Slightly broken it was discarded by its owner, who probably lived in the woods below. It is the oldest bow ever found in Europe and is now on display in the National Museum of Scotland.

Like the Capon Oak it is a tangible link back to our prehistoric woods, hewn from the very trees that once covered this landscape.

The oak, the bow, all of the woods and trees and forests across Northumbria, are touchstones to the wood culture we have all but lost. But still we love trees, woods and forests and enjoy them for their beauty.

Which naturally brings us to Kielder and other, less ancient, Northumbrian forests, with their own particular mix of manmade lakes and treescapes and wholly natural dark skies but that is another story, for another day.

*(Hownam and Morebattle,
Yetholm and Cheviots)*

# The Street

This is not 'Benefits Street', or 'Coronation Street' and quite unlike your street, it is 'The Street'. It is as far away from a reality TV show or soap opera as you can imagine. There are no houses to speak of, occupied at least, and only a few people pass along it these days crossing, as it does, rough, open hill country and prone to bouts of extreme weather.

The Street I am talking about and exploring is one of the four main ancient track-ways that connect the Scottish Borders, through the Cheviot massif, to Northumberland and vice versa. It starts at Barrowburn on the English side and steps north west, over to the hamlet of Hownam and then on to Morebattle, coming close to the largely intact Dere Street Roman road, one of the other key old routeways, going north, into Scotland.

These are the drover, merchant and shepherds' routes, the prehistoric passes of The Borders, passageways through the past and into an otherwise impenetrable landscape.

I am walking it this day from the Scottish side with my wife, Ratchel, starting at the village of Morebattle and aiming for a special hill, which lies just off The Street, called 'Sundhope Kipp', then on towards the heights of the aptly named, 'Windy Gyle'.

Before we start off, we linger around Morebattle and Linton Kirk, putting off the steep climbs ahead, but also intrigued by the history of this flat, open vale and its two obvious settlements, perched on their rounded hillocks, facing one another, either side of the valley.

Linton Kirk is another beautifully balanced feature in the landscape, a tiny church alone on its small hill, looking almost too quaint. This evaporates as you walk up to it and are greeted by evocatively carved skull and cross bones on the church wall facing you, and on the entrance side, carvings of angels, hour glasses and a knight slaying a dragon. The skull, timers and angels have innocent explanations, linked to the 18th Century obsession with symbols of life running out and turning to dust, not, as I assume, a sign of pirates or plague.

The carved knight and dragon tell of local mythology; this is said to be the one time home of the 'Linton Worm', slain by a local Saxon nobleman which, along with the Northumbrian Laidley Worm and the more famous Lambton Worm of Durham, probably gave rise to the George and Dragon stories. The worm presided over the great Linton Lake and wetlands that once covered this valley between the villages.

What sort of actual creature, if any at all, inspired these legends, can only be guessed at. We have no boa constrictors or anacondas and never did have any big snakes at all. Perhaps the bigger birds of marshes, the herons or cranes and storks, though they seem far too elegant to be seen as dragons; perhaps birds of prey like eagle or harrier? It seems most likely that these worm creatures were wholly invented, Anglo Saxon symbolic beasts, to serve a story of bravery and man's taming of the wild, our serpentine struggle with the forces of Nature.

I have never entered and felt such primal cold in a church as this. Perhaps the air is still fused with the cold, damp breath of the worm?

Lost lakes and marshlands are a recurring theme. As we cross Northumbria, from one end to the other, our awareness grows that in its past, many places were marshy and from early times to the Victorian age, we lived close to, or in these game rich environments.

Prestwick Carr, near Newcastle airport, still quite marshy, was a very extensive example and in the south of the region, around the Vale of Pickering and Holderness, there were many lakes and swamplands.

We contemplate this as we look across the remains of the lake, further down the valley, towards Kirk Yetholm, still a big marsh, which could invite a harrier or dragon, if they were about. All there is today are several heron and these entertain us for a while, before we resolve to move on up.

We progress along the route to Hownam, passing more wet grasslands and dodging tree branches brought down in the storm of the night before. In places roads and paths are covered in tree litter, junked weak and rotten limbs of old oaks and ash everywhere, as if there really had been a battle under cover of darkness.

At Hownam we join the upland section of The Street, climbing quickly from the valley to the smaller hills of the Cheviots, which envelop us as we advance. The path climbs slowly up even more rolling parts of the Cheviots, showing their softer side. Still steep though, but the day is warm and we stop for photos at the standing stone part way up, affording brilliant views.

Up we wind until we notice the embankments and ditches that mark our distant destination, three interrelated hill forts, with the distinct promontory of Sundhope Kipp in the middle.

We notice, as we walk on over the tops, distant views of abandoned farms, located in what seem today, impossibly wild places; one, in the lee of a big hill, appears totally surrounded by moor and bog, with no apparent track to it.

The route here is criss-crossed by the banks and ditch remains of prehistory and Mediaeval activity and each small hill bears tell-tale shapes of hill forts and other defences and cultivation terraces.

When finally we alight upon the highest point, we clamber onto the banks of Sundhope, which juts out onto an isolated promontory, with steep sided slopes to either side, high above the valley below.

It feels like a Northumbrian Camelot, bending the land's form to its will, dominating all it surveys. Of all the forts on hilltops around here, Sundhope Kipp keeps its haunted atmosphere; it has a rugged individualism and is a towering statement of territory.

Sitting there a while we eat a basic picnic, just listening to the wind and watching the light change from afternoon to evening, before turning silently and wandering back the way we have come.

As we do, a hare starts up in front of us and is lit by the sharp light, so that it shines gold, before disappearing off into the bracken. On the edge of the moor, there are flocks of fieldfare and redwing coming in from Scandinavia, marking the onset of autumn into winter; a few long tailed tits loop from the edge of a little conifer plantation, looking like flying musical notes, chiming above the moor edge.

It has been another day of Cheviot emptiness, devoid of people and yet we walked in the footsteps of many who had passed this way before us, over thousands of years.

Unlike any other street that we know today, this one is actually a place to escape our modern busyness, where, in the past, you would have heard the clatter of carts and the chatter and bartering of passing tradesmen and hill dwellers, day after day.

I reckon, if you listen hard enough, you can still hear the sounds of this upland melee, in the winnowing winds of Sundhope Kipp and The Street.

*(Kirk Yetholm and Wooler, College Valley,*
*Scotland and England)*

# Cheviot Machismo

There she lies, recumbent, the enormous femininity of 'Northumberlandia'; the very recent landform expression of our ancient past, rooted, very firmly, in the present. An artistic, philanthropic and corporate, industrial concept, as well as a cultural and landscape one, she radiates the relationship, between Northumbrian people and where they live.

Northumberlandia is monumental. At over a quarter of a mile long and set in a sculptural setting of forty six acres, with four miles of paths around her, she dwarves any earlier attempts to celebrate our place in the landscape. Even the Stonehenge complex and the prehistoric chalk giants of the south of England struggle to compete. She is the biggest single human landform sculpture in the world.

The site is almost on a par with some Egyptian and Central American ritual complexes. Yet most would argue she is not a ritual formation but very modern art, agnostic at best. I would say that just by the very act of her creation, the forms used and their links to the wider landscape, she has symbolic meaning.

Perhaps, because she has been made by giant mechanical excavators and mining engineers from the very spoils of the Earth they have exploited, we should attribute much less spiritual significance, but whatever the means of her making, 'Slaggy Sally' or 'Slag Alice', is made to invite interpretation. Intended or not, she is totemic and iconic and people will make of her what they will.

Her form is Celtic in design and character, a body of spirals and flowing land lines, reminding us of the ancient ways.

What, I wonder, would the wandering Celtic Christian monks of the 7th Century, the Stone Age shamans who created the famous rock art features, the Iron Age hill fort builders, the Anglo Saxon chieftains or the Romans, with all their goddesses, have made of her?

She is also a play park and a viewpoint. Rather oddly, you may stand on her breast or forehead and gaze into the near and far, a hint of coast to the right, the woods and fields and factories, houses, roads, the airport not so far away and even down into the guts of the Earth itself, the active, open-cast coal mine below her. But most importantly, you can see, on the far north horizon, the rolling curves of the Cheviots, the inspiration for her creation.

Landform artist Carl Jencks saw the Cheviots and interpreted them as a male figure reclining in the distance; he was moved, with his commission, to model a female partner for them, setting up a sort of Ying/Yang resonance across the miles, the female form of the soft lying lowlands and the masculine ruggedness of the uplands geographically connected in a big landform gesture. The rest is recent, art history.

I too see the male gender attributed to the Cheviot Hills; they are 'ripped' those hills, possessing a rounded muscularity.

Looking across from Yeavering Bell or Green Humbleton or The Cheviot itself, they appear like tightly packed muscle groups. I choose to see them as an enormous, well-honed 'six pack', smooth as eggs, on the outside, hard and volcanic underneath.

The Cheviot Hills have a habit of disappearing, one into the other. Nowhere else have I noticed this 'Russian doll effect', of one hill seeming to fit inside the curve of the next; as you scale one you think is higher than the next, it turns out to be slightly lower. In this way, one hill eats up the next, transposing one on one, like some neat hill stacking system, a hill, within a hill, within a hill, coalescing way into the distance.

While Northumberlandia lets it all hang out, the Cheviots are gently clothed in a thin, tweediness of rough grass and heather, kept shorn by their own breed of sheep, aptly called, 'the Cheviot'. White faced and well-muscled, they're the perfect, upland grazer, bred for their fine wool as well as their heather-fed lambs.

The hills have solidity and are difficult to get to grips with at first, only a few, small, no through roads penetrate their interior; they are a northern massif, though they are definitely hills not mountains, with one exception, The Cheviot itself.

The great dome of The Cheviot rises above all the miniatures of itself, as if it is protected by them. It can be scaled, or slogged to, from various points, slowly gaining height, from one steep hill to the next, until you land upon its boggy pate, its often snow-capped shine recognisable, instantly, from any vantage point.

They are surprisingly challenging for the walker and you can explore them all day and see no one, just a lot of distant sheep and the odd goat. There is true solitude to be found, a rare joy and whilst they are managed by man, they feel as wild as wild can be. They seem unpeopled and yet they are peopled. There are signs of earlier occupation everywhere, gradually sinking back into the land.

Arriving one evening at Kirk Yetholm, less than an hour before darkness, I am determined to get into the Cheviots at once. I race up from the car park, one of the few proper gateways within the hills, straight up Green Humbleton hill fort and onto Burnt Humbleton, before dropping down to the Cuthbert's Way long distance path, crossing the Scottish-English border near the Stobb Stones, momentarily straddling two countries, an ill-defined line in 'no-man's land'.

By now it is getting dark, the sense of the rippling landform fading around me into deep dusk, emphasised by the appearance of a pale smudge of light over the ridge, a moon-bow, or 'brocken spectre', reflection.

Crouching next to a wayside cairn, I watch as the white, glowing plume of moonshine contracts and expands like a living thing trying to take shape, fighting off the dark. I see a partial circular form rolling under its shroud of cloud, as if a giant ball of Cheviot sheep's wool has gathered there and is being rolled, pulled and squashed slowly by the air currents. Finally, it shrinks to a simple, pale glow, over the ink black hill.

I scramble back down the hill, the wind that has blown hard all day seems to have vanished with the moon and it is entirely still and properly dark now, so that I become closely aware of my heart, breath and each footfall onto alternate, soaked grass and rock.

The sound of the nearby Witch-Cleuch Burn is correspondingly louder, bringing to mind a beautiful close-up of a dipper I enjoyed at the very start of the walk. I watched it feeding and preening in Halter Burn, every detail revealed of its two-tone, brown-feathered waterproofs, the flicking white lens of its underwater eyelid, the crystal white of its throat and belly, as it bobbed and minced, from rock, to water, to rock. It seemed unfamiliar with humans, in any form.

A loud piercing cry startles me back to the moment and the dark sloping path. I stop and gaze sightless into the black banks of the burn to my left. More cries and shrieks, the unmistakeable sound of cats fighting, as if somehow they have been transported from a back alley. It is followed by nothing. It feels as if the sounds have not come from the ground, but from the air around me, cats flying over the Cheviots; the dark can play many tricks.

I recall, on another late return from the hills, in this very spot, I had stood staring up at the sky, trying to place the sounds of gaggling geese, passing by in skeins overhead. They could not be seen as they were flying above the clouds; then it really did feel as if the sky was calling.

I put it down to foxes hidden in the gloom, or birds even, grouse and owls often make strange sounds. But I am unconvinced; it sounded like cats fighting. Perhaps they are strays from a nearby farm?

The only 'moor-cats' I have heard about, other than the wild cats of the Scottish Highlands, were those rumoured to have been taken to Top Withins, the setting for Wuthering Heights, on the remote top of Haworth Moor, in Yorkshire, by the last person who lived there, a shepherd. They hated the environment so much, it is said, that they made their way back across four miles of rough moor, to the village. I liked to imagine how they would have looked to anyone taking the Bronte trail to pay homage: three cats in a line, chasing each other's tails across the moor, meowing all the way.

Maybe these sounds in the dark are lost cats in the night. Or, more fancifully, they could be the familiars of the witches of Witch-Cleugh Burn, out on patrol. Whatever they are, like them, I slip off, into the Cheviot night.

*To the* **Heart** *of it all, exploring Northumberland and border links*

# Northumbria-Land

The heartland of the old Kingdom and a place very close to my heart and working life. The wildest county in England and in its northern reaches so struck through with ancient and historic sites you can feel the resonance of Northumbrian spirit and culture everywhere.

This is the land of Saints, Aidan, Oswald, Cuthbert, Bede and of Hadrian's Wall, of the Great Whin Sill ridge and its castles, of Anglo Saxon Royal Palaces, hill forts and prehistoric rock art in quantity, Lindisfarne and the Farnes, Kielder Forest and Water, itself the biggest 'manscape' of water and trees in Europe, of Northumbrian hill, coast and moor. The land of border mires, moors and the rivers Tyne, Tweed, Coquet, Wansbeck, Blyth, Breamish, Pont, Rede and Glen and of more, much more.

In the south of Northumberland there is a gentler, more ordinary, rolling agricultural countryside, but it too is full of natural surprises, many of which connect through the urban fringe, into the heart of Tyneside and Newcastle.

Foremost amongst wildlife, it is the land of the red squirrel and now the red kite, the Chillingham wild cattle and goats and where otters, deer, and birds of many varieties thrive, including outstanding seabird colonies and areas of importance for wildfowl and waders.

It is just about impossible to encapsulate Northumberland as a whole, as it is a microcosm of all that is distinctive about the old and modern day Northumbria-Border-North-East. All I can do is share a few experiences from this North Country, reflect how it feels to me, through excerpts of encounters with its diversity.

*(Lindisfarne,*
*Holy Island and beyond)*

# Pilgrims Crossing

"Jesus!" I confess to taking the Lord's name in vain, more than once, under my breath, as I face the return journey of another 2.3 miles, across the sands and muds of the 'Pilgrims' Path', from Lindisfarne.

I did the whole outward journey barefoot, as tradition dictates, at the end of the 62 mile, Cuthbert's Way trail and, as I have been staying on the mainland, I face a cutting, fierce wind on the return, though the whole walk is being conducted in blindingly sharp light. It is an illuminated and illuminating journey, a personal Lindisfarne Gospel, in motion.

There is something about walking in such places which puts us back in tune with ourselves and brings out a sense of our place in the natural order.

The sensation of going barefoot on sand and mud is not familiar to us apart from the odd dip in the sea at the height of summer when abroad, usually in the company of many others. As a deliberate act, it is a return to Earth.

Feet become feelers, test for certainty on which to rest the weight; they are pummelled by the harder sand ridges and caressed by the felt-like, softer, sandy muds, cut at by the hard blades of marsh grasses and bathed and enlivened by the cold pools of briny waters. Each footfall is reacted to internally.

So I set off, following the line of poles in the sands marking the traditional crossing of the flats, aware that to stray too far from them could lead to immersion in quicksands or deep water channels. There's nothing like a hint of danger to focus the mind.

The passing of cars on the road causeway to the left soon dwindles and the feeling is then of solitary progression on a natural, blank canvas, just you and the elements. Walking several miles barefoot is a challenge but can become a walking meditation. You feel an empathy with the footsore Saints of old and pilgrims who still tread this path, seeking their transcendence.

Footsteps in sand are symbols of our evolutionary pathways. Looking down and seeing the bare feet of others, a smaller graceful female mark, the heavier ones of a large man, I am reminded of those I have seen preserved in the peat just down the coast at Hauxley. Here there are Stone Age hunter gatherers' spoor alongside those of the animals they were after, the extinct aurochs, wild boar and red deer, the first Northumbrians.

Even more poignant, having recently visited the British Museum, are the exhibited Happisburgh footprints from Norfolk, discovered in 2013 and only preserved for a short time, the playful ramblings of a family of proto Sapiens, nearly a million years old, the first Britons. Our bipedal lives really are written in our footprints in the shifting sands.

Back in the moment, I approach Lindisfarne. It is a good, fine day, despite the wind. But it is hard going. Saint Cuthbert and his Celtic Christian clan on their spiritual walkabouts in the Northumbrian wilds did not have the convenience of 'the Pilgrims Coffee House' in the village, or of modern day windproof clothing. But then it was suffering they sought and the chance to take on Nature.

The draw of Lindisfarne is as obvious now as it was then and even earlier. It is a place apart, a world in microcosm, a natural retreat. It is both beautiful and bleak; it can be a place of physical and spiritual challenge, if you choose, or a pleasant place to reflect.

It was the perfect, eastern, seaboard 'Iona', from where Aidan was sent by Columba, in the 6th Century, on a mission to establish a new Northumbrian monastic centre. He followed many who revered this part-time, tidal island, its special spirit of place recognised from early times.

It is a 'liminal' place, perceived as having only a thin veil between you and your god. You can still feel this, even on a touristy day when you find a quiet corner to muse, your own temporary hermitage. The Pilgrims' route is but one way of encountering the wild inside yourself.

What I like is the feeling of containment you get on the island; it has a sense of timelessness. To be here, for me, as on Iona itself, is to be in a continuous state of spiritual awareness.

It also has a distinct shape. I think of Lindisfarne as the 'curlew island', approached along the long bill of its causeway to the oval of its main island skull; the Priory is its eye and the little bays of its coastline form the crenulations of its now old, worn cranium, breaking back down, slowly, into the sea.

This may be fanciful but it seems appropriate to think of it as ornithological in morphology, as it is a focus for bird life all year round, something Cuthbert recognised and celebrated. The tale told of him immersed in freezing waters being wrapped around and warmed by otters is an image I like to reflect upon. Nature and person naturally combine here.

I spot a merlin, perched motionless on one of the pilgrims' poles, as if a portent of the dangers beyond. I have watched many rare birds fallen here on migration. There are the 'cuddy' and other sea ducks that harbour here in the worst of weathers; you never know what will turn up. A pair of the piebald, long tailed duck made my day this time.

As I walk on across the sands I see lines of waders, dunlin, knot and a few larger curlew feeding on the edge of the retreated sea, silhouetted like tiny kinetic teeth, reduced to black lace, in the mudscape.

I become constantly aware of the seals, their mournful, mewing calls carry on the wind, their up-curved bodies stranded in the distance, splashing and playing in the running waters. They are the watchers and the keepers of the seas around the 'lindis' (Celtic for 'land').

Nowhere is more Northumbrian than this Holy Island. It is a condensed form of northern spirituality of place, made of people's interaction with wildness, over thousands of years.

To walk, barefoot the Pilgrims' Path and to follow Aidan and Cuthbert's ways, from The Borders to this isle of tranquillity, is to re-anoint yourself with the essence of all that is, Northumbria.

*(The Fell Sandstone)*

# *Blawearie*

The sheep keep the grass short on this knoll, a green island, in a sea of moor and mire, in the lap of the Northumbrian Sandstone Hills. It and nearby Old Bewick Hill, sum up the long lived in and characterful northern hills.

On this turfed rise stands a romantic scene, so unlikely at first, it seems purposely composed, for picturesque appreciation. It has all the symbolic overtures of a 19th Century Friedrich painting, complete with rocky outcrop and wind-distressed tree and ruin.

A decrepit farmstead, with two pointed gables, stands at the right end of the hillock with a tor-like crag to the far left. In between, there is a scatter of windblown, spiky trees. You might think it a film set for a ghostly tale. But this is not contrived, it is a first encounter with Blawearie. It has its own stories to tell.

Blawearie means 'sick of the wind' and you can see why it deserves this label, being miles from anywhere and bleak and miserable on a winter's day, harsh in a blizzard. But it is a beautiful and convenient hideout too and a cosy place to hole up, to live within the land, undisturbed. It is a place that beckons and demands to be revisited.

Even without its back story (more of that in a minute) it is a privilege to come across this out of the way place, with its perfect symmetry, an accident of human occupation and Nature, showing so well the interaction of both. This interface of human and natural order is at the centre of everything that is Northumbrian. The Sandstone Fells and this place lie testament to this unwritten law, standing perfectly spaced, between the high Cheviots and the lowland coast.

Signs of people occupying this land for thousands of years are scattered everywhere across the fells and yet they retain a feeling of wilderness.

Just sit for a moment among the old ruins and listen to the piping of the whape (curlew) and plover and it is as if the land itself is singing to you. Notice the smell of the peat you have walked through to get here, the five-toed imprint of a 'heath badger'. Gaze across furze and rushes at a rough and unforgiving tapestry, where birds like the ouzel, meadow pipit, the wheatear or 'old white arse', merlin and kestrel feel at home.

I first found Blawearie while searching for rock art at Old Bewick hill fort, on the slope facing the abandoned farmstead. At first I thought it must be a folly, but close inspection revealed it was real enough. I looked into its official past later, after soaking up its atmosphere and making my own mind up about the place.

Many might feel it is ghost ridden. I find it to have been once loved and revered and it has a gentle and welcoming feel.

Growing out of the two weather sculpted outcrops, there are rhododendrons and other garden plants, introduced by former occupants, and two trees remain of the old orchard, a greengage and a bullace. There are tiny steps between levels, giving the impression of a once tended garden grotto. In fine weather, it is the perfect place for picnics and becomes an oasis among hills.

So what is its human story? It was built about 1840 and lived in for over a hundred years, as a steading in the hills, where a shepherd could easily live amongst his flock. Many families lived here with their children, all walking downhill to school, whatever the weather, at Old Bewick hamlet, about two miles away .

It was the family home of the Rogersons until the 1940s, when it was commandeered by the military to practise shelling. Still it survived and must have been reoccupied as Mr and Mrs Faill were recorded living there in 1946, perhaps until the '50s. It was abandoned after the occupier was finally overcome, having been snowed in for weeks. Living in this isolated, 'out-bye' land had come to an end and Blawearie fell into poetic ruin.

Human occupation of this site, or very close by, goes back much further. Just before you enter the farmstead, on your left, there is a well preserved Bronze Age ring cairn, a 'filled in' stone circle enclosure of large stones, with a central burial chamber. It was excavated and restored in the 70s by teacher turned historian and archaeologist, Stan Beckensall and it revealed some high value items. There are twenty more burial cairns within half a mile of it. The Bronze Age cemetery commands great views of the Cheviots and is, like the house, in a natural basin between hills.

Even older, sculpted over 5000 years ago, are the rock art motifs, carved on boulders around the Iron Age hill fort at Old Bewick, across the way. The fort itself is impressive, in fact the only double hill fort in England. From the air it looks like a giant pair of double rim spectacles sculpted into the hill top.

Different abstract patterns and combinations of these symbols are found on other crags and hill tops all across the Sandstone ridge and right down to Simonside near Rothbury, the widely acknowledged 'sacred hill' of prehistory.

This area of Northumberland is the classic place for these intriguing, but little understood, Neolithic symbols and Stan is famous for finding and describing thousands of them. Similar carvings are also found in similar environs, as far south as Yorkshire and in Argyllshire, revealing that ancient Northumbrian kinship with the west again.

I like the local word, 'ringses', which perfectly captures both the concentric banks and ditches around hill forts and other ancient enclosures, as well as carved 'cup and ring' patterns. Circles, within circles, seem to be replicated at all scales in Northumberland, as seen again, in the round sheep folds, so characteristic of the hills and other features.

At Blawearie itself, on top of its crag, some modern day chiseller has copied a cup and ring into the rock. Its freshness and clarity show just how striking they would have looked when new, revealing the pinkish colour of the fresh cut rock and its obvious 'out of place' presence, also emphasises that their positioning was carefully selected and meaningful.

The big rock at the top of a pasture on the shoulder of Old Bewick, which looks across to Blawearie, is particularly dramatic. It is a massive erratic, left by glacial ice. Its sloping surface is covered completely in rock art motifs, a series of cups and rings and multiple rings, some squashed up against each other and with long grooved tail-like channels, running downhill. There is a large, natural but enhanced basin, with an obvious spout, full of rainwater, at the top and many subtler patterns only just visible.

On one occasion I saw the old stone 'come alive' and it left me with an inkling into how these patterned rocks were supposed to be experienced and what their intended symbolism could mean.

It is a grey day in the hills, cloudy and drizzly, after heavier rain, as I climb the track from Old Bewick Farmhouse and approach the big slab of decorated stone. I lean up onto the edge of the rock for a better look, to try and decipher again the pictographs, some highlighted by their wetness, but the light is flat and unhelpful.

Just then, the clouds break and for a minute or two the rock is illuminated by streams of sunlight and at once the whole thing seems to make sense; it is one complete and intricate design, of interconnecting shapes and signs. The combination of wetness and light make it shine and almost move. It looks like a landscape in miniature, with the grooves and tails turning into imagined streams and rivers and pools. The inanimate has somehow become animate.

The show isn't over. After a while I walk backwards, away from the rock, keeping my eyes on it, until I cannot make out the marks and as I do so the slab is revealed in full colour. A short, intense rainbow moves across from the left and shines on and through the rock, striping it in its spectrum. I can picture the rings and grooves almost lifting off the rock and becoming part of the stripes of the rainbow itself, sky and rock becoming joined.

This feels like a series of truly magical moments, with me interacting with a dynamic landscape. I can't help thinking that this is what was intended, a ritual focus in a whole animated land, which people felt part of, where every natural sign held significance.

No one will ever know their purpose for sure, but excavations around them in Scotland hint at ritual practice and veneration of rocks as sacred, ancestral, territorial signposts, places of shamanism and of connection between soil and soul.

There seems good evidence for their involvement in water veneration. They could even be the symbol of raindrops as the life giving essence. Whatever their origin and function, they and their places, are still special and draw our primeval curiosity.

North Northumberland is evidently now, as it has always been, a place to lose and find yourself in the landscape, a place of easy communion with natural forces.

(Hartlepool, Northumberland, the Dales,
Cumbria and the Borders)

## *Red Squirrel Country*

In the 1990s I used to joke that there was nothing as rare as a red squirrel in Hartlepool and I was talking from experience. I knew then how endangered they were, having found an isolated colony in a wooded dene near the town and was unsure how long they would survive.

Red squirrels have become icons of the efforts to conserve northern wildlife and like many other people I have become part of helping them endure.

Their story, one of being displaced and taken over by a hostile invader, being pushed further and further north into their border heartlands, is a very Northumbrian story, reflecting the waves of human displacement that have created its culture.

Perhaps that is why they draw our empathy, as like human Northumbrians they appear to be survivalists of character and individualism. Moreover red squirrels are an indigenous link to the wildwoods of our ancient past. We have lived with them, on and off, at least since the Mesolithic and longer in Europe. They, like the badger and other natives, are bound up with our cultural heritage and our emotional connection to the wild.

My parents remembered seeing red squirrels where I was brought up near the Tees Valley woods of East Cleveland, in their youth, but by the time I was interested in wildlife they had been replaced by the grey squirrel invader, which easily out competed them for food and habitat, at least in mixed woods and broadleaves and carried a pox virus lethal only to reds, which was not known at the time.

Whilst some coexisted for some time, pox could take out a red colony in a couple of weeks. By the 1970s you had to go further north to see them. As a child they were merely fictional, playing the parts of Squirrel Nutkin in childhood tales and Tufty, the only ever road-aware red squirrel.

Meantime I got used to and enjoyed the grey. Like any squirrel they are cutesy and photogenic and I loved their acrobatics in the tops of the big beech trees in Riftswood, Saltburn.

My first actual red squirrel encounter was in the Yorkshire Dales on an A level geology field trip to Ingleton Falls. Stopped in my tracks, I remember vividly the equally startled animal, poised, like a red and white star, on the side of a smooth-skinned oak. We saw more later and I was hooked. There is something so graceful and minimalist in the movement and shape of a red squirrel, ergonomics in motion, that they are irresistible. They have a grace and fluidity that only the mustelids and the felines get close to.

After that I saw more on holiday in Scotland and the Lake District, where they were still very numerous in the 1980s but in slow decline. As a student I watched them on prime Nutkin territory at Far Sawrey, the home of Beatrix Potter. I even saw their almost black, melanistic versions in the Swiss Alps on holiday, very odd looking, as if by some misfortune they had been creosoted!

My Hartlepool squirrels were enchanting. As ever, it is the unexpectedness of an encounter that was as thrilling then as it is now, that helps cement an experience in the mind.

A researcher had given me the nod that red squirrels were in Thorpe Bulmar Dene, just off the A19, near Elwick and following his instructions on where he'd seen them, I took the path into the woods and down to the dene itself, loitering awhile on a small bridge. I was convinced I would not see them. My guide had himself only brief viewings and was unsure if they were actually resident or just passing through. But it was a warm, early Saturday morning and there were plenty of birds about.

I crossed the bridge and there, sitting only a few yards away, in the middle of a hawthorn bush, eating berries, was a perfect and rather filled out red squirrel. I watched it for some time as it did not appear to be bothered by me, intent on filling its face. Eventually it and I moved on and turning right I followed the path into a mixed wood, with some high canopied larch and beech. I was delighted to see, through binoculars, several reds running around in the tree tops and could not believe my luck.

I revisited the Dene many times and was not often disappointed until gradually over a few years they were hard to pin down and then not present at all. It was then I saw the grey squirrel for the first time there. It was a shock and a painful realisation, that you seemingly could not have one with the other. At that point no-one had yet proved the suspected pox virus connection, but their disappearance seemed so dramatic and quick. The reds had gone from Hartlepool.

As I developed a career in conservation in the North East, I saw this happen all over. Cumbria and Northumberland remained the strongholds of reds but their distribution even here got fragmented and localised.

As I write this, efforts to turn this around by targeted culling of greys in red/grey areas and other tactics seem to be working and, for the first time in 100 years, perhaps the red is coming back, though Hartlepool is not to be re-colonised anytime soon and it is a pipe dream in most of Durham and Yorkshire, where greys are so firmly established. Accept and enjoy the grey seems the only strategy there, if you can.

Royals, several charities, many devoted community groups, intent on keeping their reds, private, Government and European funds and landowner partnerships are all being brought to bear. It is as if the whole of the Northumbrian armies of conservation are working to uphold their flag-bearing, red squirrel as an emblem and mascot. For many it is a totem animal with which they feel a special bond.

I am glad to support this and am encouraged by signs of success. But, like many, I feel challenged at having to kill any animal, even to safeguard a native. The alternative is too high a price. The red simply cannot be lost; it has become so much a part of the identity of place.

Every time I question the approach, which is only holding the line until non-lethal methods of control can help, I rest my case on the many beautiful encounters I still have today with the mesmerising red squirrel. Somehow this speaks for itself.

From Wallington to Kielder, from Woodend to Blagdon and Plessey to Bassenthwaite and from Grasmere to Eshott to Penrith to Whinlatter to Formby to Grassington to Alnwick, I see red squirrels and delight in their being. I have seen them eating, playing, mating and fighting. They never fail to entrance.

They are not to be idolised though. They are wild animals, not just cartoons. I have been reminded of their rodent viciousness when one attacked me as I was refilling windowsill feeders, (blood everywhere, and mine!). They exhibit all the bad behaviour we are offended by, including digging up bulbs and lawns, barking young trees and occasionally disturbing young nestlings, of which we are not so forgiving of the grey. Not so long ago they too were shot as 'vermin', evidence of the changing values we attach to species.

For me the red squirrel is important and beautiful for its own sake, a piece of our heritage in danger of being neglected or ruined and lost forever.

So, saving our squirrels transcends the logistical and moral arguments for conserving them for me; they are part of the red blood of the north, which we must try to keep as the natural integrity of what constitutes Northumbria.

*(Kielder and other Forests)*

# A Skyspace

Is this what it's like when you die, I wonder? A short, white tunnel into nothingness, ending in a universal chamber, a thoroughfare to the stars?

I am sitting overnight in the 'Skyspace' installation in Kielder Forest, created by international artist James Turrell. It is a sculptural building which functions as a focal point to observe the sky. It is designed to make us look up and outwards, but it also helps you look inside.

Part chambered tomb, part observatory, part kaleidoscope, it is a theatre of light play. It has a church-like quality too.

It may be a manspace, an artscape, but at night it is overtaken by Nature. For the place in which it sits gives out an energy. As the sky and forest become the show, this architectural construct turns into a performance place, to notice the subtleties of Nature. You contemplate your part in the bigger picture of Kielder and the universe.

Kielder is unique, being the biggest, planted forest in the land, framed around the biggest, manmade lake in Europe. This is a land made by rearranging the building blocks of the landscape itself.

But the strange thing is, Kielder feels natural, like it has always been there, despite being industrially planted with exotic conifer. It has absorbed the qualities of wilderness, partly by its sheer remoteness, its upland attitude and its size. This is a big place: big forest, big trees, big water, big skies, which at night are uniquely dark and at all times tranquil. The sky rules over the trees at night. It is a bigger entity than anything we can create, but everything here demonstrates the enormity of the universe of which we are just a tiny part.

All forests have an element of natural, broadleaf woodland and a range of other habitats, not just trees. There are many important, open spaces too. This is what makes them forests; they are landscapes with a feeling, when you are in them, of boundlessness.

Forests are part of my being. I started my career in the 'real' forest of the Forest of Dean. This has been forested continuously since prehistoric times and was one of the Royal Forests established and managed as the King's hunting preserve, where gentry could hunt deer and boar, in mediaeval times.

It retains this atmosphere and its diversity. It performs all the services of a modern forest, timber, recreation, biodiversity and art, yet it feels deeply old and authentic. People there still refer to themselves as 'Foresters', a race apart, inhabiting 'The Forest'. Yet it has also been replanted and changed since its wildwood days, so that it is a very mixed forest today, with some conifer areas not unlike Kielder.

You couldn't re-create this sort of forest in the hills of Northumberland. Kielder is the right forest for its environment and even though it is very new, by comparison with the Dean and other age old forests, somehow their structural elements have been transposed here.

This is also true of other, smaller versions of Kielder across the region, such as Hamsterley Forest in Durham, and Dalby and Cropton in North Yorkshire, the smaller Guisborough, in Cleveland. All of these feel 'natural' and 'wild' to a degree when you are in them.

This struck home when, one September day, under the tall conifers of Hamsterley, a friend and I came across a mouth-watering scene; as far as we could see were hundreds of the highly valued mushroom, the cep, boletus edulis, the penny bun or porcini. I had to admit, this was a better haul of edible fungi than I had ever seen anywhere, even in The Forest.

Forests are full of surprises but they also have a lot in common; a forest is a forest is a forest. The only exceptions are treeless forests, like Dartmoor, but we won't worry about them!

Art installation is also a big thing at Kielder. The forest provides an enormous outdoor exhibition space and an interaction with the natural world. The sculptures too, tend to be big and bold and modern, a giant, carved, wooden head with mouth agape, brightly coloured, metal shelters and many more. Skyspace, the newer Sky Observatory nearby and all the sculptural projects here are 21st Century monuments in this artfully contrived, landscape masterpiece.

At first sight, it seems the efforts to 'capture' and define the dark skies of Kielder is the last attempt to manipulate the sky, as if, having fixed the land with our hands and eyes, we need to reach up and move things around up there too. But thankfully no, the emphasis is very much on accepting and enjoying the natural movement of planets and skies, the one element we can't easily change.

It is the place to see stars alright. And as I walk up to the Skyspace site in the gathering dark, on a warm, moonlit night, I am guided upward by the calling of one tawny owl after another and the wind chasing and chanting in the far off treetops. It really feels like I am the only person for miles, because I am.

Is it safe to enter, I hesitate? You can't help feeling irrationally apprehensive on first creeping into this great burrow. What's inside? What is waiting? Those primordial fears, like entering a chambered cairn of our ancestors.

But this rounded chamber is womb like, hard but nurturing, cradling the sky which bears down on you from the circle in the roof, a distillation of night sky. Skyspace brings all that vastness of sky to a point of intensity, straight above your head.

It is hypnotic even just observing the movements of the clouds. When, at dusk and dawn, soft, coloured light shines around the rim of the aperture, as if from nowhere, you sit within your own 'aurora borealis'. The feeling of otherworldliness is profound.

It is a meditative circle and as I sit, I hear each breath taken up by this giant instrument, assimilating my body rhythm and turning it into a circular song line, resounding around the giant bowl. Just the occasional drip of earlier rain emphasises the cave-like quality. The wind and trees whisper along the lip of its night mouth, making it hum.

It is a Zen like setting, a Taoist design, circles within circles, clean lines of black and white, with discs of golden sun, sheer moonshine, star shine, the halo on the hill. I am 'between Heaven and Earth'.

Exiting Skyspace brings an even greater appreciation of empty space, of the pure brightness of the whole sky, not just a part of it. No longer contained, I feel spat out, suddenly minute, which is indeed just what I am: a small moving collection of fundamental particles, made up of the stuff I'd just been watching so intently, yes, stardust, of course.

*(Haltwhistle, Chollerford, Birdoswold and other high spots)*

# Wall

A grand gesture for a grand landscape, defined by human ingenuity and determination, is the landmark that is Hadrian's Wall. Not just any wall this, but still a wall, it is regular and constructed, stone upon stone, with joints and layers, a squared off shape; it retains moss and lichens; it has a rubbly interior, a hard chiselled exterior. Apart from the Great Wall of China it is surely the biggest wall there is.

But it is also a divider in time and place, a gesture of power, perhaps fear: a boundary in a hard, raw place, a place to contend with and complement the geological abruptness of the Great Whin Sill ridge. It is that almost impossible thing, a man-made geological feature on a natural one, and equally as uncompromising in its adherence to the landform.

Up it climbs, down it rolls. The Wall flows with the contours on the big dipper of the scarp, on which it sits. Then, in gentler places between, it strolls across fields, hides in woods and shimmies past farmsteads. Its forts are no more, its camps decamped but, as the map shows, there were as many as five in a couple of square miles. This was a densely inhabited place in Roman times: an inhospitable line of life, linking one coast to the other.

I have been visiting Hadrian's Wall since childhood, when, like many, I developed an obsessive interest in all things Roman. I remember staying in the posh George Hotel at Chollerford as part of a bargain break, luxury combined with first impressions of all the Roman sites. My first glimpse of Brunton Turret was from the road nearby and how excited I was to see this massive, broken-down wall asserting itself still on the valley side, advancing on the river.

It has become part of my own landscape memory of Northumberland and since then I have walked and seen most of it. Every bit has a memory or meaning: the scale and position of Housesteads: the humanity of Vindolanda with its preserved leather shoes and shards of notes from everyday people living everyday lives: the appearance of it along the military road with its vallum and other defences: little forts in hidden away areas: the bit by the roundabout off the Newcastle bypass.

If I had to pick a favourite stretch I would go for Birdoswald, just inside Cumbria. It is amazingly complete and many of the fort buildings are visible, every element of Roman life on The Wall is traceable. This section of The Wall is long, high and impressive, at one point almost violently throwing itself up and down the hill towards you.

I love too the negative or concave shadow to the wall itself, the lakes or loughs along it and in nearby countryside. There are four in all, managed as nature reserves, as they have special plants and insect life, as well as birds. Crag Lough, the smallest but perhaps the most dramatic, lies under The Wall as it undulates over the exposed Whin Sill. These have an Arthurian feel to them and appear fathomless and ancient, perhaps giving rise to the legend that, at least Broomlee Lough has buried treasures in its depths. They are simply glacial scrapes, but they are beautifully wild, upland waters, somewhere in character between a loch and a tarn.

This night The Wall has lights again, as it once had every night along its milecastles, turrets, camps and forts. Today it is lit by human imagination and memory, by a need to celebrate time's passing, the power of millennia concentrated into now. I am one of hundreds of volunteers posted every mile along its length to mark its 1600th anniversary. Just for tonight, I am a lamplight legionnaire.

The burners are lit, the mile by mile points are marked by them in the growing dark, flares and candles in between, mirroring the stars. When the lights eventually go out, darkness falls around us, as does the silence of reflection and a sacred truth that comes from the ambience of our interaction with this transient corridor of light along the Great Wall.

Lost in our own thoughts, perhaps we sense the ghosts of Roman mercenaries at their posts, empathising not so much with their battle with their northern foe as with their life in this harsh place, this edge land, its constant wind and chill. There is a sense of linkage to points beyond, in both directions, The Wall pushing on ceaselessly from one outpost to the next.

The Wall is over explained, an icon and almost a cliché. A world heritage monument, it retains a mystery, a quiet excitement. Yet is just a 'wall'.

Before the lighting, the murmurating starlings try to steal the show with their own undulating display, a gradual joining of flock upon flock together into one flowing, curving mass, a wave above rock and field, and a waft over The Wall, streaming and diving, a headlong windsock of birds, thousands moving as one, before dropping, without notice, into trees.

We go to light the beacon and as we do, we look up and notice again a pure white wedge above the horizon. We take this to be cloud until we realise it is actually the back of Cross Fell, in snow, like a pair of rounded Pennine shoulders shrugged against the icy wind.

Here on The Wall, it is a sharp, cold but beautiful night and we have the comfort of the burners, which we light and stand around.

In the wood near our burner, site number 23, just up from Cawfields above Haltwhistle, there is a hidden portion of Wall. At first you don't recognise it for what it is. Forming the path edge it is easily taken for an earth bank. But Hadrian's Wall shines through the thick vegetation that shrouds it, well-shaped regular blocks visible in places beneath the thick briar, moss and ferns.

There it is, four feet high and thicker, almost forgotten about, hiding its light under a bush, waiting perhaps to be exhumed or hopefully left alone. This piece of Wall is left in peace for the moment, for the weasels to live in and the deer to gain height on. It is being slowly reabsorbed back into the land.

The rest of The Wall is illuminated tonight for nearly an hour, along its length, the first time for 1,600 years; beads of light shine out to heighten the momentary spectacle, disappearing into the dark distance.

*(Goatscrag, Northumberland, Highcliff, Guisborough, other high spots)*

## *Look-Outs*

When fictional caveman 'Stig of the Dump', with his modern day friend Barney, passes through some form of time warp and ends up at 'the great gathering' of his Stone Age people, all assembled for a night of ritual revelling, he becomes intoxicated by the momentousness of the event. He goes into a trance-like state and with the others starts dancing and hallucinating, living out his prehistoric past in the present, with Barney getting caught up in his excitement.

Just about anything then can trigger vivid memories of these moments for Stig: an old flint, a standing stone, a pattern on a quarry wall. The present day and the imagination are very mixed in the mind of this cave boy caught in the 20th Century.

I can empathise with Stig. In fact it doesn't seem to take much for me, either, to become transfixed by the feel of a place or object, its echoes of the past still tangible. Certain locations and landscape features vibrate with the past and I imagine myself there in a different moment. I also have to confess to suffering a little from 'Golden Age Syndrome', imagining that, far off in the past, times were much better than now, more natural at least and part of me craves to be back there, though I know in reality it would have been incredibly tough to survive. This nostalgia comes upon me in the higher places that have changed little over time.

Across Northumbria, there are locations at heights that lend themselves to looking out across the landscape and it is easy to visualise their use in the deep past. These are key points of ancestral download for me, what I call 'look-outs'. From scarp ridge to hidden caves and rock shelters to table top hill, they are the watch points used for thousands of years by people, to observe the ever changing patterns of land, sea and sky.

These are the places to watch the sunset and rise, the journey of the moon and stars across night skies, the play of cloud and shadow on the land and the weather that has such a bearing on the North Country. These inspiring look outs give an age-old insight into the Northumbrian mind-set and our relationship with its natural history, past and present.

Yeavering Bell, hill fort of all hill forts, is one such place. You don't need much imagination here; it is laid out for you. But it is a steep climb and a bewildering place of goats and ghosts, encounters, sounds on the winds, a haunted look out.

Climbing up here, it is hard to see why people actually lived within its walled enclosure in Iron Age times. It is a defensible place alright but also cold, open and bleak, even on a sunny day. Having walked from one hill top to another, from Hare Law to the Wester and Easter Tors, by the time I get up here I am glad to lie on my back and watch the clouds pass over. I am collapsed among the fallen rocks used as a wall around this ancient fort cum clan base.

Today it is re-wilded, only a few humps and bumps to be seen, as is the case on nearly every hill hereabouts. But this was the most important. I share it with crows, falling out of the sky like black silk handkerchiefs, poking their jet bills between boulders.

There are sheep aplenty but also one more distinctive compatriot, a wild goat. This is highly appropriate as Yeavering means goat in Old English: this is 'the hill of the goats' after all. This one is a large, scraggy individual with impressive horns and a back like a teased out rag rug, a mix of black, brown and white, a confusion of patterns and textures, as if it has picked up bits of the landscape and welded them to itself as it has gone along. I wonder why it is alone as they are usually in small groups. It stares at me with satanic eyes but a baleful expression. I stare back, wondering how long its kind have been living here. Could they be as old as the fort itself? It looks it. I scramble back down. It stays there, every bit the hill hob, guarding its ancestral site.

The best of the natural lookouts has to be Goatshill Crag, in north Northumberland, on the Fell Sandstone ridge. It is close to Roughting Linn waterfall and its famous rock art outcrop. This is an obvious and well-used, natural, rock shelter and a place to watch the landscape below. Coming up here, I feel I am not just walking in early man's footsteps but taking on his persona. I am 'Stig'.

I can't help mimicking ancient actions, as if I am actually watching the herds of wild beasts below; I trace my finger in the rough stick-like rock carvings of deer, crouch on the ledge gazing outwards, imagining the scene from thousands of years ago. I imagine fires being lit and hunters exchanging glances as flames flicker and they pass around meat to chew and heather brew. Even the TV explorer and backwoodsman Ray Mears played hunter gatherer here. It is just as if the bison and elk had been taken away recently.

Earlier I chatted awhile with the man who farms the land just beneath the rock shelter. We talked of the changeable weather, the hidden dangers of the distant Cheviot Hills, he in his gentle, lilting Northumbrian dialect, which seemed to fit with the soft flowing landscape here - me in my grating, out of place tones, conversing as people have here for centuries, about much the same things. We didn't mention the rock shelter or the rock carvings, or the past, only now really mattered.

Much farther south, in the Cleveland Hills above Guisborough, the same landscape arrangement is found. I'm standing at Highcliff Nab, a big, square block of a rock poking out of Guisborough Forest. It is like coming up to a volcanic plug, but as you get closer it is obvious that this too is sandstone, weathered into a series of shelves and hollows and, at the front, a shallow overhang and flat platform.

I realise I haven't been up here since I was a kid and for some unknown reason, I feel a lump in my throat and my eyes well up. Perhaps it's just being here again, a sense of re-connection. It certainly has a grandness about it, a real beauty, as you stand and look across the land below. I guess I can't work out why I haven't visited it more over the years, like some old, ignored relative. I know friends who run up it every morning. I have seen it in the distance many times, but never thought to climb it. I have let it become a backdrop. What else might I have done the same with?

High emotion in high places isn't unusual. In fact they invite profundity and beauty sometimes invites release. Once settled, I remember what I'd read of the thousands of flints found here under the crag, by earlier excavations, the remains of flint knappers getting their spears and arrows ready to hunt the game below, when the fields of Guisborough and beyond to the sea were prairies for herds of wild beasts.

It is harder to imagine than being at Goatscrag or Yeavering, with the bypass and the town, the hints of Teesside's industry in the distance, but somehow Highcliff retains a significance that rises above it all.

The past is more tangible here in Northumbria than in most other parts of England. All we have to do is find the right place and, like Stig, close our eyes, tune in and take a walk back in time.

61

*(Beaches and shores of Northumberland)*

# Druridge

It's April Fool's day and I'm looking down from the dunes onto Hauxley beach. It has been raining heavily but now the sun has broken through the hanging mist, so that slowly the scene develops in front of me from soft highlights into super high definition. The result is a picture so illuminated and sharp it feels hallucinatory.

In the distance, the dark blue and white of sea frames the foreshore of rocky, sandy, watery textures. The tide is so low you might wade out to Coquet Island, just floating there offshore, on a raft of mist.

From the dunes above, it is an abstract picture, composed of all these elements and the forces of refraction and reflection: a world of briny microhabitats of rock, pools, seaweeds, sands and muds. Only at its very edge is there any movement, turnstones turning on the tide.

In the middle of the darker, jagged rocks and linear, bedding planes of turquoise, purple and buff, lies an ovoid of pristine sand, as big as a five-a side pitch. I feel drawn to it as to newly fallen snow. Barefoot, I step onto it, feeling its trampoline texture, taut as sailcloth, rippled at the edges.

On days like this you feel glad to be alive, a moment when you feel the connectedness of all things, the 'overview effect' described by mountaineers and astronauts: pure joy.

This communing with Nature on beaches goes back a long way and is the essence of the Celtic Christian tradition and Paganism. It's also the foundation of Taoism and other universal theories. It inspired Cuthbert, Aidan, Bede and others to set up home in the Farnes, Holy Island, Alnmouth and South Shields, all places of shifting skies, sands and waters. In Northumberland we are truly 'blessed' by beaches.

Unspoilt sands run all the way up the coast from Blyth to Berwick, with Bamburgh, Ross Sands, Beadnell and Newton, Seahouses and many more top of people's lists. Of them all it is on Druridge Bay that I find some of the most rewarding.

This seven mile long crescent of sandy bay, from Hauxley in the north to Cresswell in the south, exhibits the diverse qualities that make beaches so special, from their rocky promontories to their long strands of uninterrupted sand.

They have a moodiness, a sense of isolation and raw wildness, calm one minute, raging the next, always invigorating.

They are places of birds and wildlife. The mix of rock, sand and mud are the habitats of wading birds like curlew, dunlin, oystercatcher, knot, sanderling, redshank, and ringed plover. At Cresswell and Seahouses you might catch the purple sandpiper which lives up to its name in bright light, its yellow legs complementing its purple sheen. In winter, snow buntings feed on the dune marram grass, whilst, at any time, offshore you might see gannets, auks, seals, or glimpse a dolphin or porpoise.

I recently discovered, on a special outing with Northumberland Wildlife Trust's 'marine dream team', that one of the best ways to feel the power of Nature is to visit a rock pool at night. Without the colours and shades of day, these pools and their rocky foreshores become massively textured monochromes, metallic and shiny, the water silvered by torchlight beams and sky reflections. In between probing beams, unseen creatures move the oil-like surface of stranded sea. Momentarily illuminated, thousands of normally sedate crabs and periwinkles glide around constantly.

In daylight you can search out the amazing variety of rock pool life, maybe five species of crab, including the uncommon porcelain variety, hermit, spiny, shore and edible type or small fish like blennies, butterfish and shanny. There might be something new washed in on the tide, like a sea potato or sponge.

If you want to experience the alchemy of ecology and geology you could do little better than gaze across the raw sands and foreshores of Northumberland. All life is here and then some.

*(Alnwick and Chillingham)*

# *Looks Could Kill*

You can't see them and mostly they can't see you and that is how they like it, thanks. 800 years of isolation behind a wall in a park woodland of their own, not interfered with by people, has made the Chillingham cattle not only the rarest of breeds but by far the grumpiest.

It's the way they look up at any human visitor who joins one of the regular safaris to observe them from a safe distance. 'If looks could kill', as if on first sight the big bull is saying something to the effect of 'I don't believe it, not another intruder, haven't they got anything better to do? Get out of my park!'

These cows hate people so much they will kill their own calves if they have been touched by one, so hands off, not that you are likely to get that close. But they are softies inside surely, I hear you say, don't judge a book by its cover. They look like big, huggable teddy bears with a bit of attitude. Well no, they aren't actually, they are aggressive, wild cattle.

They are built like Ninjas, smaller than normal cattle but packed with muscle, having the effect of making the head look even bigger by comparison. Their expression is serious, judgemental. Their sharp horns are devil-like, their sunken, dark eyes, malevolent, while their bulky, white bodies appear angelic. They chew away unaware and unaffected by the aesthetics of Man.

Chillingham Estate and these cattle are both an enigma, a time capsule from the 13th Century when the cattle were first enclosed by the Grey family (of later Earl Grey tea fame) along with wild boar and deer for hunting, a larder on the hoof, safe from the early reiver rustlers.

They are their own species, self-managing out the sick and weak, in charge of their own ecology. They are just about a hundred now in a walled estate in north Northumberland and a few kept secretly in Scotland, to preserve the bloodline, if disease should threaten. It amounts to a Northumbrian eccentricity, a time warp in action.

Having lived in seclusion for so many years, like an evolutionary experiment, they are akin to pre-Roman forest cattle, the aurochs and early cattle captured and bred by the first farmers, from which they probably inherited their white bodies, red ears and great horns, ( made to point forward in males and backward in females). They may also have been kept for ritual sacrifice by ancient peoples.

Even Darwin visited them to observe a distillation of his theory of natural selection. The unavoidable inbreeding of their small population imparted an 'island effect' of gradually making the cattle smaller by comparison with their wilder ancestors. Small but very powerful that is.

This explains their different behaviour from domesticated cattle. They act more like deer, organised into small herds with their own King bull, hiding their new born in thick cover like fawns, the bulls fighting each other for the right to breed, often goring each other badly in the process. Even the females are covered in the scars of battle. They breed all year round and are always ready for a fight. So watch out.

For a large, heavy-hoofed animal they are surprisingly agile and can run and jump over bushes their own height, an adaptation of their need to run from their natural predator, the wolf. Even pregnant females have an adaptation to tuck their unborn young under their ribs and run for it, if need be. They can live up to fifteen years.

Down the road in Alnwick, despite first appearances, the 21st Century has arrived. The medieval, market town is still partially walled and centred around the castle seat of the Duke of Northumberland (evidently they love walls around here). Ancient buildings are adapted to modern lifestyles.

There are café bars and Wi-Fi connections; people are digitally networked and all shopping needs are catered for. Our penchant for gardening for pleasure, is impressively celebrated in the grand parklands of The Alnwick Garden. Despite the modern veneer, you can still visualise the time when the cattle were first captured.

But all of the change since then has passed the Chillingham cattle by. For them there is a sense of continuity back to the prehistoric wildwood which covered this land thousands of years ago. As 19th Century Alnwick naturalist, Luke Hindmarsh, observed in 1839, this is where 'aboriginal cattle' thrived alongside bears and wolves, boar and beaver, all of them long extinct, apart from these feral cattle. It is remarkable that they have survived.

Grumpy they may look, grumpy they may be, but they are just self-assured, proud to be stuck in Northumbria's deep, wild past.

To the human observer, they are a reminder of what we have lost and gained in those hundreds of years. Perhaps we are living within walls ourselves, of another kind?

*(Whin Sill and
other geomorphologies)*

# Geo-Logic

I well remember the words of Ernie Bradford, my Sixth Form geology teacher and mentor, emphasising that the piece of rock I was examining closely was 'tholeiitic basalt, not just basalt, mind, tholeittic basalt, related to dolerite.'

An old school field geologist, Ernie expected you to know the detail and if you couldn't answer his searching questions, you felt as if you had let him down terribly. As a consequence I learned off by heart the texts we were set.

If you do look this rock up in a geochemistry or mineralogical text book, it will describe the unique recipe of the igneous intrusion that makes up the Great Whin Sill. Does it matter? Well it does help to know what is under your feet, as you walk the Northumbrian ways. Ernie always underlined that you need to know your rocks if you are to have any hope of understanding how the world works and why it looks like it does, anywhere.

It is interesting to reflect that the whole genre of geology was born and refined between the two poles of Northumbria. James Hutton, the 'Father of Geology', was an Edinburgh geo-scientist of the 18th Century who, through studying the rocks of Arthur's Seat and other formations throughout the North East and Scotland, proposed the very ancient origin of the Earth, recognising it was formed by deposits of materials, over millennia. Likewise, William Smith, another founding father, later used the Jurassic coast around Scarborough to cement ideas of stratigraphy, the notion of layers of rocks sequentially representing different ages. The Rotunda Museum there is dedicated to him.

Likewise, the Earth Science visitor centre, 'Dynamic Earth', is appropriately situated at the bottom of Arthur's Seat, where the history of geology and geological processes are graphically explained. Their earthquake and volcanic eruption simulation is memorably physical. Just now and again we get a real jolt and I have several times over the years experienced a Northumbrian tremor. The rocks are alive.

Even in humble Hummersea, near Loftus alum quarries, the young Lewis Hunton worked out, in his very short life, that each horizon in the rocks could be relatively aged by its 'zone fossils', before dying tragically of TB at the tender age of 23. Obviously he was put on this planet just to find this out and his amazing discovery, expressed in a one off paper to the Royal Geographical Society in 1836, two years before he died, is his legacy, what is grandly called today, 'biostratigraphy'.

This also meant he had worked out that the fossil ammonites he studied had slowly evolved, twenty years before Darwin's theory of 'The Origin of Species', making him one of my Northumbrian heroes. Having collected these same fossils myself, for years, they feel as much a part of the fauna of Northumbria as the gulls that sit on the cliffs where they are buried.

It is as if the landscapes of Northumbria had been set up as a giant, outdoor classroom for Earth Scientists, its concentration of geo-morphologies are so intense and diverse.

The Whin Sill is a good example of this, as are the Yorkshire coast, the Tyneside and Durham coalfields, the Cleveland Hills and other ridge lands which lay out their origins, like a book.

The Sill forms a ridge of hard rock which stands like a backbone running across Northumberland from Hexham to the north coast, diving underground in the middle. On spurs of it stand the icons of our heritage: Lindisfarne and Bamburgh Castle, Dunstanburgh and the Farnes and most obvious of all, Hadrian's Wall. It was pushed up through layers of Earth by a Cheviot centred, volcanic event in the Carboniferous period, before coal was laid down (about 295 million years ago). This flat bed of magma welled up and crystallised to create an important land feature.

To the early Northumbrian, it was an invitation to enhance its natural boundary-marking tendencies. This was a geological, big act begetting a big, human reaction. Wherever natural forces created a particular upstanding feature, a rocky crag, a distinctly shaped hill, a high ridge with rocky pillars, our ancestors made them into functional and ritual touchstone points; the rocks 'spoke' to them of their importance of place, perhaps the work of their gods or ancestors.

Throughout Northumbria the synergy of geology, landform and significance of place for people is so obvious you could call this imperative, 'geological determinism'. Ernie would have liked that, the rocks seen as being in control.

Borne of fire, the Sill ridge soon became a cold and barren place. Its elevation in northern climes brings a salty blast of North Sea air, even in summer. But landform and microclimate coalesce to create the particular bleak beauty that we know as 'Hadrian's Wall Country'.

The Sill is not alone in its class. Geo-intrusions are not uncommon and it has a smaller cousin in Durham, the 'Little Sill', a precursor of the bigger intruder. It also has a more vertical, ridge-forming relative, the Cleveland Dyke in the Tees Valley that runs alongside the pinnacle known as the 'Cleveland Volcano', Roseberry Topping. But this came all the way from the Isle of Mull much later than the Whin Sill rocks and it has a more andesitic, acidic composition, like the volcanics of the Andes, back to the old text book!

There are other spectacular, ancient, volcanic and igneous landscapes around the UK and the world, like Scotland, the Lake District or even Dartmoor with its great exhumed batholiths of granite, which originated as enormous reservoirs of magma below the Earth's crust.

Farther afield, in the Massif Central, in France, or the amazing Garatoxa region in Northern Spain, you have wonderful, re-vegetated 'lost worlds' of obvious, old, volcanic cones and craters. You only need to go to Iceland or Italy to see Earth forming activity today, including new sills and dykes, like those of the Whin Sill complex, exuding in swarms and nests.

I have sought these places out, seeing Etna in full lava flow, climbing up and looking into the volcanic crater of the tiny Sicilian Island 'Vulcano', whose classic shape made it the model against which all volcanoes are compared.

But while their high drama is unforgettable and inspiring, I return to the Whin Sill and its brethren, with a better appreciation of their deep time origins and subtleties of natural processes.

More than this, there is a feeling of respect and belonging. For there is nothing that more epitomises the region of my birth and home than the Whin Sill. It and the Cleveland Dyke are the epitome of North Eastern-ness, not just geographically, but in other ways too. Their hardness, beauty and strength in the face of adversity and the timeless qualities of wildness that this brings, sing out Northumbrian human strength of character.

Thus, it is the land of the border shepherd and hill farmer, in former times the land of Roman auxiliary, prehistoric coloniser and Pictish Scot, reiver, early Christian Saint and Northumbrian King. On top of this, it has a deeper, spiritual atmosphere, hard to define.

What better place to put a castle than Lindisfarne, Bamburgh or Dunstanburgh? These are not just defensive positions but symbols in the landscape, feeding off the power of the Sill itself.

Just now, a multi-million pound visitor centre is to be built, at Once Brewed, near Hadrian's Wall, looking up to the Whin Sill and Roman sites. 'The Sill' project will become a centre for the study of all landscapes in the UK. You could hardly have a more appropriate place for it. No wonder these 'geo-scapes' are a tourist Mecca. After all, tourism is a modern form of landscape worship.

The Sill has a human heart at the core of its hard, old body, linking it to the very origins of the Earth itself and reflected in the hard exteriors, but soft, welcoming hearts of its people.

*(North Tyneside, South-East Northumberland)*

## Water and Witches

With its black, cowled head, fiery red eye and orange feather headdress the Northumbrian 'water witch', or black necked grebe, is unmistakeable. Their nickname originates in America and has been adopted by some locally, who recognise their almost satanic looks; close up, that red eye and strange, almost grinning expression make them look 'possessed'.

These are rare birds too. Only about forty pairs breed in the UK as they are on the extreme western edge of their European range, so we are very lucky indeed to have a few of these fascinating birds in Northumberland. They inhabit loughs, lakes and big ponds, where they find their favourite plant, the amphibious bistort, to feed and breed around.

This plant in itself is rather lovely, a water based version of the common bistort, better known in the north as dock, or 'Easter Ledgers', as it has been foraged for years as an edible human treat. Its amphibious cousin is not so tasty but it does form a pink sheen when in flower, across the water bodies it grows in. It supports and attracts the many insects and small fish the grebe loves to eat and also provides a mat of interlocking fibres that help hold up the fragile nests of the birds. It is a synergistic if not a symbiotic relationship between bistort and bird, there being a lot more in it for the grebe than the plant.

The water witch pops up in some odd places. As well as the more remote loughs and lakes in Northumberland's wilder parts, it favours those particular ponds which are seen across the urban fringe and old industrial areas of the south east, formed by subsidence from coal.

There are hundreds of these. Around Cresswell Pond, itself a great example, there are over a hundred of slightly different type and size. Studied by Northumbria University, they have a unique ecology of European significance. Few are favoured by the grebes, which are rather picky.

No wonder then that the ones where the bistort grows are often the haunt of the water witch. So in the midst of urban Tyneside you can watch these birds getting on with their slightly mysterious lives. They are prone to disturbance though, to the extent that actual locations where they live, are not advertised so you will have to do your own recce if you want to see them. My nearest ones are accessed via a supermarket car park.

On this particular July sunny day, I am watching them with their mature young, with birder in the know, Steve Lowe. There are three pairs and they seem to have offspring floating all around them. Almost as big as the parents and furry black and white 'greblings', they refuse to dive and depend upon the frenetic fishing of their parents, the big babies.

Another ornithologist friend, Ian Armstrong, has studied them for years and told me they are prolific egg layers, a response to their need to be able to refill nests that are often predated (otters can wreak havoc) or are washed out. Their nests are very deep, with the cup sitting often below water, so that the eggs are always wet, just out of reach of a passing pike.

They also have the charming habit of carrying their small young on their backs, amongst folded wing feathers, formed origami-like into a nursery pen. Ian describes watching on several occasions, in horror, as without warning the mother bird dived underwater with her full brood and popped back up moments later, with all still attached. Her wings had just moved slightly as she dived, creating a canopy for them, and they seemed unperturbed.

The birds I am watching are a little big for this and so I can't experience the same views but it is entertaining to see families of grebes playing and feeding with purpose, growing into miniature, portly versions of their parents. I also have a chance to look even more at the adults. They are stunners in design and plumage. They could be the Audrey Hepburns of the bird world, so elegant are their necks and heads. Their black plumage is satin, their eye a burning ruby. Those strands of orange feathers, that form great eye appendages, shine golden in the sun and bristle in the breeze. Their slightly upturned bill, the bouffant headdress, neat, russet sides and easy buoyancy stand out as diagnostic features and make up for their weird air.

When they aren't feeding they appear serene, demonstrating the art of 'Wu Wei', or effortless action, floating in their grebe zones. This is in sharp contrast to their feverish and strange courtship at the start of the breeding season. Then the birds follow one another and synchronise their moves, rearing up out of the water and doing a dance as they move their necks snake-like, whilst bristling head feathers and lifting their wings.

As well as in Northumberland, I have seen the black necked grebe in Scotland, one in particular, off the coast of Iona, after stormy weather. It was utterly alone and looked lost and out of place. I was struck again by its strange beauty. Its golden feathered brows were blowing upward and back to form a sort of New Romantic quiff. I wondered if it had been picked up by the storm and whisked away, far from its Northumbrian mate!

Watching the water witches, back on Tyneside, dreaming in the warmth, I begin to reflect on water and witches, of one sort and another. Water has always been seen as a dynamic and transparent element, one that might afford passage or insight into other worlds and dimensions. It is the stuff of witches alright, the plaything of spells and potions.

In and around Haworth, in Yorkshire, folklore tells of the 'water wolf', a mysterious creature, that lives in wells and springs and if consumed will suck up the nourishment from any living thing, man or beast, until they shrivel and die. There are many remedies to rid you of the water wolf, said to be induced by the curse of a witch.

Day dreaming of water, witches, and wolves, just some of the strange things I have come across in my wild Northumbrian quest. The water witch is one encounter I will seek out time and again and the water wolf one I will seek to avoid.

*(Gateshead and
other roundabouts)*

# Magpie Architecture

Like bunches of mistletoe, the magpies' large, domed, hollow sphere nests of intertwined sticks and branches cannot be missed, as you drive along the trunk roads into Tyneside and Newcastle and most of our northern cities and towns.

Magpies start to construct roadside nurseries well before the leaves appear and they last for ages, are often topped up and re-used and re-designed, extensions fitted, becoming territorial homesteads. A magpie's building habits are the nearest we get to the African bower and weaver birds and their amazingly complex nest constructions. They have adapted so well to our urban landscape, they are part and parcel of the green infrastructure of our towns and highways.

These nests are noticeable and appear in unlikely situations, such as in the top of a single isolated tree, squeezed between the flyover and the old soup kitchen, in central Newcastle, or, massive, in a tree in the middle of a paved university campus.

Sometimes they are the only reminders of Nature amongst the urban detritus, the concrete and asphalt, apart from the hemmed-in street trees themselves. I am always catching them out of the corner of my eye, vaguely circular, unlikely structures, often given away by the jerky movement and undulating flights of their black and white feathered weavers.

These giant, woody baubles, a mess of twigs and branchlets and found objects, as diverse as a scarf or a McDonald's carton, are fashioned by beak and claw. Sometimes two or three in one tree. They remind me of how Australian Aborigines depict tree canopies, as umbrellas of circular florets. This claw-crafted bird basketry looks too perfect, intricate and well-made not to be the work of humans.

They may be as big as a basketball or larger, have a distinct canopy and bowl of a nest, connected loosely or they may be a large ovoid, tightly wound around. They can have an annex or a satellite, no planning permission required.

On the A19, between the horse paddocks, urban fringe and the grim concrete construction that is Gateshead roundabout, there is a good selection of magpie avian architecture. In the semi-rural, field edges, against the background of piebald ponies, these woody globes are spaced out along the sparse hedges and surviving sycamores. One is perfectly placed in the arms of a self-seeded apple, which glows with blossom in spring and golden fruit in the autumn.

My favourite is in a lone, ornamental cherry, in front of a crescent of council houses, up from Heworth Metro Station, where a traveller's van and truck are usually parked. Trapped in the traffic, I look and wonder. Perhaps they are attracted, not just by the convenient nest site, but also by the glinting chrome of the caravan, for all corvids like shiny things.

In its tall branches, magpies have built a huge twig ball, with its own separate additional canopy, and there are two smaller spheres above it, loosely connected, like granny and teenage flats. Often, there are several birds in excited attendance, I saw seven on one occasion, 'keeping a secret'. It could be a magpie community centre.

Further along, close to the roundabout, lies another sort, a circle completely enclosed within a large hawthorn bush, only properly visible before the leaves come on. As they do, the mesh of closely twined branches converge around it, absorbing it, until it looks impossible for anything to get in or out and is hardly visible. Yet this hidden nursery often has a proud bird perched on top of the bush or moving about inside, adding more material.

Now you have read this you will start to notice the work of the magpie everywhere. They are in hedges and trees all around us, as we share the same suburban habitat.

The birds are often seen and can congregate in large numbers, with over twenty birds flying into well-established night time roost sites, such as the big hawthorn scrub area around what are called 'brownfield sites', ear marked for development, very often the most biodiverse bits of town. For me, the abandoned, re-vegetated football pitches near Grangetown on Teesside and the unofficial buddleia forests along the Tyne towards Blaydon, come to mind. Magpies are often the most noticeable birds because of their size and plumage. They appear mostly unconcerned by people.

Many people though bemoan magpies' success in our human centred, denatured environment. They see them as 'lucky' or 'unlucky' birds, or just plain predatory, taking over their gardens, bullying the smaller birds as they feed, or they don't see them at all. But I admire their iridescent black and white looks and their creativity. They are part of the urban scene of Northumbria and to my mind are a welcome reminder of the adaptability of Nature, in the same way that I enjoy watching foxes and red squirrels in Gosforth Park, the elusive Ouseburn otter, seals, waders and herons on the mudflats of the Tyne.

Surely magpies should be appreciated in Newcastle of all places, more than anywhere else and be given celebratory, almost sacred status? For it is here that the widely worshipped local football team, Newcastle United, has adopted them as their mascot, presumably, in recognition of their artful, winning ways.

*(The Tyne Valley
and Tyneside)*

# A Pet Corncrake!

Anyone who has heard a corncrake in the field, perhaps in the western isles somewhere*, will certainly agree that this is one bird you would never give house room to. Their loud repetitive 'creck-creck' call is amusing and atmospheric outdoors, but under your desk or bed, it would be a nightmare.

It is, then, a person of singular character, who can tame and share premises with this noisy, partridge-like, bird. It gives quite an insight into Thomas Bewick, the 18th Century Northumbrian naturalist and his passion and determination to get to grips with Nature that he did indeed keep a pet corncrake. In fact it ran about his house for some months, becoming unusually tame for such a secretive bird.

Bewick produced some of the best woodblock print illustrations ever made at his modest farmhouse at Cherryburn in the Tyne Valley and in his later home and studio in Newcastle. His well-researched, descriptive and anecdotal, picture filled books on animals and birds were the foundation of the field guides we see today and offer a unique taste of daily life in the country of his time.

I re-visited the cottage of his birth and childhood and the farm next to it, where his family lived right through to the 1930s. Owned and managed by the National Trust, it is a hidden gem of a place and an inspiration to all who are excited by natural history. Like all the best corners of lowland valley English countryside, it is quaint and homely with an everyday rough beauty.

The farm is set in rolling hills near Ethringham Common, on the slopes of the Tyne, surrounded by trees and fields and with streams where Thomas loved to fish. Ash trees line the beck behind the house and a big, old pollard stands in the field nearby, which was probably there when Bewick was.

I arrive, on a sun-drenched, early autumn day and it is as if scenes from Bewick's vignette woodcuts have come alive; a young man is chasing an escaped sheep across the yard, watched by a donkey, whose knowing expression seems to say he'd seen it all before. A lady beekeeper tends black bees, a traditional variety Bewick would have been familiar with, but rarely seen today. Butterflies take to the wing, speckled woods and red admirals. Blackbirds and thrushes attack the early fruit in the orchards, much as they and many other birds would have done more than 200 years ago here, becoming his life's inspiration.

Cherryburn is a beautiful time capsule, the perfect place to stop awhile and contemplate the Northumbrian mind-set and just take in the day.

So that's what I do. I take a seat and soak it all in, gazing down the wonderful Tyne Valley with the river invisible in the valley bottom below, but where I remember I had watched, from Stocksfield bridge, otters playing in the river just a few miles upstream from the city, as if I was in another world. I recall many other sightings up and down this valley, even a red deer stag, crossing a corn field, not far away, a very unusual sight and probably an escapee. The weather and the atmosphere, the pure quality of the whole setting, could not feel more pastoral and Romantic today, preserved, more or less, as it was in Bewick's day.

I picture the young Thomas Bewick running around the garden, chasing his passion, perhaps examining birds and animals he wanted to draw and later with more purpose, using live specimens, (like the corncrake) to work from. He captured their forensic detail in drawings, then carved them into fine grained boxwood, for block printing.

His was a rare skill, his prints are works of art, reminiscent of Japanese netsuke, especially so in his fine depiction of trees and foliage. Some of the intricate work revealed on close examination is just miraculous, they are so tiny and accurate. It was one thing noticing such details in the first place, another entirely to capture them, at such a scale, in rough materials and by candlelight. They remain today, little blocks of inked wood that shine with the life of their subject.

It seems to me, as I look around and enjoy the sun and the scene, that Northumbria is just the right place for such a naturalist engraver to have lived and become enthralled: Bewick, who became the Northumbrian Wordsworth or Clare of carving and illustration.

In Northumbria, we are always subliminally in touch with our natural selves, partly hidden underneath our urban veneer. This can make us individualists, Thomas Bewick, for one. He described himself as exhibiting 'the overflowings of an active wild disposition'. This manifested throughout his life in his outgoing attitude, his big natured approach and of course his eccentricities. Who keeps a corncrake in the house for goodness sake!

The Tyne Valley is not the wildest part of the region at all. It is undulating countryside of woods and fields and rivers. It feels unspoilt, though the hand of man is everywhere. It is a semi-natural corridor, a gateway to the raw drama of Hadrian's Wall and the Pennine hills, eventually Cumbria. But it is a graduated introduction, where history combines subtly in a linear landscape and where all the things we might expect to see are present, like the otter, woodpeckers, badgers, deer, foxes, weasels, herons and redwings, all the myriad of creatures Thomas Bewick illustrated for us so well.

It was never just fields and trees about Cherryburn and the Tyne

Valley of course. Industry crept in and Bewick's family worked a coal mine as well as a smallholding. Downriver, in Newcastle, nothing short of an industrial revolution was happening at the same time as a revolution in people's fascination with all things natural. People were discovering Nature, in all its diversity, trying to identify and understand its detail and how they related to it.

They relied on observation and recording of their local environment. It was also the age of the great, gentlemen naturalists and wildlife collectors, such as Bewick's southern contemporary, Gilbert White, Vicar of Selborne. They watched, collected, illustrated and theorised, sometimes accurately, sometimes naively, without having the overview provided by the evolutionary schemes of Darwin to go by, as yet.

From Cherryburn I drive into Newcastle, which is where Bewick went to work from the age of fourteen, bringing his interest in Nature to town. I get there a lot quicker than he would have. I am on the industrial park at Blaydon in about twenty minutes. From rural 18th Century idyll to mega modern cityscape in no time, as if the past has been wiped out along the way.

Then I turn off and see the Tyne flowing strong towards the sea, a living waterway right through this urban centre, bringing with it a taste of wild Northumbria. That Northumbrian juxtaposition was at work again, people and the wild rubbing along together, shaping one another, by turns.

On all my journeys thereafter, across the North East, I keep Thomas Bewick in mind. To me he has become the embodiment of the Northumbrian naturalist and is a continuous inspiration.

His was a free spirit and I share his urge to observe, capture and convey the true beauty and value of our natural world. Even in the harshest places, Nature pokes through. You don't need to be in

Cherryburn or on the high fells to feel it. Thomas Bewick's prints are a reminder of this, captured memories, full of humour as well as observation.

You could say that you might indeed take the man, Thomas Bewick, or any of us, out of Cherryburn, or any piece of countryside we love, but you could not take the effect of Cherryburn or that countryside, out of him or us. Wild Northumbria will not be suppressed, wherever you happen to end up.

*corncrakes are now very rare outside the Hebrides and southern Ireland due to changes in agriculture.

*To the **Heads** of it all, venturing into the Pennine tops and Durham lowlands*

# Bishops-Land

Crossing the Tyne, we enter the Wear catchment and touch the Tees. This is the land of the three, main rivers of north Northumbria. Each of these brings a difference in culture, landscape and wildlife, even three ways of playing football; we are tribal still, defined by our riverine associations. The rivers are also important wildlife corridors, connecting the seaboard to the Pennine highlands, the lifeblood of the land.

From the table-topped, geological gem of the North Pennines, approaching true wilderness, to the Durham coalfield countryside of scarred and restored land, down to its often unnoticed but spectacular coast, there are marked contrasts in feel and experience.

The bleak, raw wildness in winter on the Weardale and Allendale tops, can give you a taste of the Ice Age and yet there is subtlety on a warm, June day in a 'magical', magnesian, limestone meadow in Durham's lowlands and wandering the wooded ravines around Durham, Sedgefield and the Derwent Valley.

The Land of the Prince Bishops, historically a Kingdom within a Kingdom, and, until quite recently, defined by its coalmining communities, is part of a middle belt of biodiversity as we progress southwards from Tyneside and Northumberland. Certainly it is just as touched by the same influences we have seen further north, with Durham a sacred centre and the last resting place of Saint Cuthbert.

There are alpine floras and places of remoteness, bird and botanical specialities. It is a part of Northumbria that I am still getting to grips with but where I have had moments of joy.

*(Alston, Halsteads, Bamburgh,
Durham coast, near Rothbury et al)*

# *Meadowlands*

I'm no botanist. The filigree detail of plant identification and their Latin names are a barrier to my understanding, making me look to the sky and woods for birds and mammals instead.

But even I appreciate a good meadow when I see one, or am impressed by an uncut road verge full of unusual species, or a sward of blue and red viper's bugloss on the dunes. Sometimes the beauty of wildflowers can stop you in your Northumbrian tracks.

A damp, coastal, wildflower meadow got my attention one summer and I try and return every year about the same time. It is delightful and only as big as the average front garden and sits between two bungalows. It presents a simple colour mix of five main flowers: yellow, pink, purple, white and mauve, against a background of vibrant green. Squint your eyes and it becomes an Impressionist painting.

Field buttercup and ragged robin, with a good sprinkling of northern marsh orchids dominate: towards its margins and in the damper areas, the deep, shining gold of 'king cup' marigold. The cuckooflower, a Liberty print, has a softer presence. Only silverweed, daisies and a triangle of horsetail fern and grasses seem otherwise to be tolerated. Now and then an oystercatcher wanders through, its black and white sharpness illuminating, by contrast, the different species.

In other places it is only one or two flowers that stand out: a whole field or bankside of cowslips: an interweaving of pignut and bluebells: a river bank, woodland clearing, with metal enriched soils, covered in tiny wild pansies: rare, upland hay meadows and magnesian limestone grasslands: unique Whin Sill plant assemblages. It is the variety over weeks and months that is breath-taking, almost too much to absorb.

Indeed, the more you look, the more you see and I find myself now 'collecting' meadows and plant experiences that capture local differences in soils, geology, landform and use, marking changes from one end of Northumbria to the other. It is a lifetime's occupation and I wish I'd started earlier.

The best way to get to know flowers and plants, just like identifying fungi or insects, is to go out with an expert, a patient one, who does not mind too many obvious questions, such as, "What's that in English?" My botanical mentor on occasion has been Dr Angus Lunn, one of Northumberland's plant experts, for over sixty years, a true botanical Elder.

Angus and his wife Jean, have their own outdoor botanical classroom, a hay field on the edge of the Pennines near Alston, on the farm where Jean grew up and which they 'transhume' to every summer. It is a floral paradise and as well as meadow, there is a rich tapestry of ancient woodland and riverine habitat. It is a microcosm of Pennine upland, apart from peaty bogs.

The field is our focus today. It is late June and the hay meadow is half grown, knee height, another month and it will be grazed off. Angus has recorded 130 species in this meadow. It would have been cut by hand scythe annually and the hay crop would be valuable feed for stock, but there is no real call for this now and many landowners, including Angus, are paid to manage their hayfields as traditionally as possible, to maintain their dwindling rarity for conservation's sake.

These hayfields are a cultural as well as botanical feature. Without ever being ploughed or fertilised and regularly cut or grazed, they provide some of the most species-rich grasslands in Europe.

All this is obvious as we walk and examine the little paddock between old stone walls. I lose count of the names and stories behind every plant Angus and Jean show me, but note some and am reminded of others. Every plant has its own back-story, relating to its niche and its relationship with land and people, often revealed in their colloquial names.

These include the melancholy thistle, sad perhaps because it has no prickles. But it has leaves green on top and white below, earning it the local name of 'fish belly': the great burnet, standing like red lollipops amongst the grasses might be 'signed', their blood redness indicating their use in Chinese medicine (as Di Yin) to help clot and cool the blood: wood cranesbill, an ancient woodland plant at home here too, known also as 'Odin's Grace', their lovely purple petals used to dye Saxon war cloaks and believed to protect the wearer.

The list is long: quaking grass and devil's bit scabious, mountain pansy, field woodrush, pearlwort and globeflower re-introduced by hand by Angus and Jean. This, like all these Pennine fringe hay meadows, is a library of 'flora Britannica', a living heritage and beautiful in its effortless complexity.

Impressive in a different way are the so called whin sill grasslands, the flora that ekes a living on the thinly soiled outcrops of the Great Whin Sill, which gets in your boots along Hadrian's Wall and around the Northumbrian castles. They are unique, as nowhere else do you find quite the same geology, aspect and microclimate.

These igneous rocks were eroded to form 'cuestas' or scarps, running crests across the landscape. Less than twenty sites remain of these assemblages, reduced by two thirds since the 1980s. They have been over grazed, or under grazed, with gorse allowed to colonise and even sprayed off with herbicide, so that what is left is even more valuable: the floral jewels in the crown of Northumberland.

They are characterised by flowers such as rock rose and lady's mantle, wild chives, maiden pink and my favourites, the long stalked cranesbill and squill. Part of their attraction is that they vary so much from site to site and the distinct differences between the coast and the hills, on the same rocks. These flowers respond sensitively to the twists and turns of the Northumbrian landscape.

Talking of looking in detail, my botanical eye and knowledge is even more limited when it comes to bog plants. They are tiny and incredibly diverse. A visit to Butterburn or Bellcrag Flow is to experience Nature at its wildest in upland England. These peatscapes are cold, wet bog-prairies, blanket bogs not, by and large, fed by ground water, but rainfall. They form part of a giant mosaic of bogs in and around Kielder Forest and the Northumbrian-Cumbrian borders, the Border Mires.

There are 55 separate bogs, covering nearly 3000 hectares, a lot of bog! Hours of work has been spent in their conservation and restoration by volunteers and organisations, over the last fifty years, after first being recognised by Angus. It is back breaking work creating dams to block the 'grips' or drains and removing trees put in by the Forestry Commission since the 1920s for timber. Standing up to your calves in the bog, you feel like a tiny piece of the soaking wilderness. It is unnerving, as if it could suck you down. The diversity of plants close up though is some compensation, the rare, large heath butterfly and dragonflies too in summer.

Whilst the idea of extensive bogs does not at first appeal, on a bright day they do look beautiful. Angus has described them as 'gloriously textured and coloured' and he is right. They are extremely 'natural' too, ungrazed, unpolluted and unspoilt.

Ford Moss, in the northern Sandstone Hills, is another bogland, a lowland, raised-up bog, made by thousands of years of peat accumulation: a fine-grained, metres deep, vegetative record of time. Framed by woodland it seems but a featureless soggy plain, way into the distance. The only vertical here is the incongruous, brick chimney from an old coal mine. From its spoil heaps, you can gaze across and take it all in.

Carefully splodge into the bog itself and the carpet below you comes alive with colour and pattern. Luminous green sphagnum moss is a framework into which patches of cranberry, cross leaved heath, bog asphodel, cotton grass and many more are set. Of the plants found here, one is insect attracting and one is insect repelling: the 'flytrap', red cushions of round leaved sundew, ingests all insects that stick to it, whilst bog myrtle's strong scent keeps insects at bay.

All these bogs are great for reptiles as they can regulate their body temperature quite easily in them and there is plenty of food. There are more slow worms about than people think. These shiny legless lizards are a treat to see, but I try not to pick them up, as they can shed their tails.

I have had many encounters with our only, venomous snake, the adder. Snakes are not everyone's first like, but there is something primal and attractive about them. Recently, I came across one coiled up in the side of a damp path, just a couple of metres away. It was enjoying the sunshine and I could clearly see its grey green skin, garnet red eye and darting tongue; then it started to uncoil, extend and flatten its neck, like a mini cobra. I admired the diamond tessellated pattern along the length of its back as it slinked toward me. I kept very still; it got closer; I stood still; it got closer; I stepped back. It glided past me, as if I wasn't there.

Farther south, in Durham, there are the 'magnificent meadows' of the magnesian limestone, clothed in mats of rare flowers, some still supporting the Durham Argus butterfly, now extinct further north. With their rock rose, dropwort, bee and other orchids and bloody cranesbill, they are also of national significance. They are found in small, re-vegetated, old quarries and on the Durham coast and reflect again the uniqueness of their geology.

There are so many distinctive plant and flower assemblages across Northumbria that you could make a Northumbrian wild plant pilgrimage your whole focus. I might also mention the Ice Age tundra flora of Upper Teesdale, with the shows of 'alpine' flowers like the unique Teesdale violet, spring gentian and bird's eye primrose around Cow Green Reservoir. These will always stick in my mind, as I recall the red faced anger of the warden there, many years ago, shouting at me and a friend as we looked for these rarities to tick off: it was a shock alright, but served to emphasise their vulnerability and rarity.

Also, I think of the wet grasslands I have enjoyed down the East coast, such as the orchid-rich roughs of golf courses by the sea around Seaton Carew: the 'seas' of hybridising marsh orchids at the Gares of the Tees estuary: Lindisfarne with its unique dune helleborine and then all the swamp and wetland specialities of the Humber head levels, which, mostly, I still cannot hope to identify or even get close to. Many floral mysteries and discoveries remain for me across this land.

What I have discovered is that plants and flowers present a fine, floral fabric to wild Northumbria. It pays to take them seriously and seek them out. Their microcosmic, highly locally distinctive worlds are a colourful way of getting to grips with the bigger picture of our great landscapes.

*(Upper Teesdale,
Cow Green)*

## Tupperware Frogs

There were thousands, yes thousands, of tiny frogs the day of the school trip to Cow Green, in Teesdale. Up they popped as we walked the bogs and followed the boardwalks that traversed mile upon mile of wet peat mire. Many of us tried to catch them in our hands as they zinged into the air. Nearly everyone was yellowy gold in colour, like chewed toffees, among the bog pimpernel, sphagnum and sundew.

They were a welcome diversion, as the day itself was soaked through and we gradually became sodden, moving like mobile bits of the vegetation through the landscape. Wetness became the theme of the day as we added to our plight, falling deliberately and accidentally into streams and pools. We were wet anyway, it didn't matter, at first.

We had been impressed with our first sight of the gigantic reservoir, a flooded valley that might feed Teesside's hungry industry and thirsty people. Its sheer scale was enough, but the audacity of man taking it upon himself to make a lake like this, where Nature had determined should be a valley, stuck with me even more. Were we really in control?

It was downhill all the way from there on, literally, as we dropped down the side of the dam and looked at Cauldron Snout, a man-enhanced long cascade, amazing. We were on our way to High Force downstream, a classic waterfall, famous across the North and one which we were excited to visit.

It was however a lot further than we and teachers had expected and were prepared for, the weather a lot worse. At least we had the gear, boots, waterproofs and of course ample provisions. Most of us though had eaten our lunch on the way there and so we were not only wet and increasingly cold and tired, we were hungry! The best school trip ever was changing to the worst, as we squelched along.

The frogs were our saviour. There is something about small children and amphibians that is a fatal attraction. Kids love frogs and newts. Even in the 21$^{st}$ Century they do, when they are allowed to. Counting the frogs, catching the frogs, chasing and minutely observing the frogs became an obsession. There were all sizes and a range of colours, from green to almost white and as big as a hand, or as small as a finger nail.

We admired their black beady eyes, subtle stripes and speckles, their tiny fingered feet, just visible ear slits, their compact bottoms which seemed to contain springs we couldn't see however hard we looked.

It was this and the rush of snipe lifting from the bogs and the glimpse of a wet peregrine on a cliff face that sustained our efforts, though we complained.

We got there, in the end. High Force was spectacular, what with all that rain. But we were desperate to get on the bus.

And before the tiredness and motion sickness kicked in, there was just enough time to open our Tupperware boxes and liberate the many tiny frogs we had gathered as we walked and which we could not bear to leave behind.

*(Riding Mill, the Derwent Valley,
Gibside, Wales)*

## Red Kite Overhead

I never thought I'd see a red kite in Gateshead, even less over the Metro Centre. They always seemed to me symbolic of the wilder areas of Britain and not at home at all in an urban environment.

One of the most thrilling experiences I had as a young birdwatcher was being let into the secret of where to see them in their native habitat, the remote Welsh wooded valleys, their only breeding places at the time.

Living in Gloucestershire it was a shortish trip to a hamlet in the mid Welsh hills, called Rhandirmwyn. Great views of these fantastic and rare raptors were to be had and we marvelled at their agile manoeuvres, their russet red plumage and cream coloured heads, most of all their twisting, forked tails. Even more satisfying was being able to watch from the bay window of the pub as one flew slowly and confidently up and down the road outside.

These days you can simply get on the Red Kite Bus from Gateshead centre and alight near Riding Mill, or Gibside in the lower Derwent Valley, passing the Red Kite pub on the way, stopping to sample its red kite menu. Later you might follow the red kite trail to a likely viewpoint, where you can see several birds at close range.

They are not so rare now since the success of reintroduction schemes over the years and are a common sight on the motorways through the Chilterns, on the edge of London, in South Yorkshire and in other locations where they have been released and monitored and where they are often supplementary fed on carrion and farm leftovers. We almost take them for granted.

To see them in these everyday settings, floating over housing estates, visiting people's gardens, viewed from a roadside, seems strange but in fact kites were always birds of the town and were common in Shakespearean England, when they helpfully cleaned up the garbage-filled streets.

Being natural scavengers and actually one of the laziest birds about, they like to loaf around rubbish tips and reliable places of easy pickings, not doing a lot of preying at all. The odd one does go for a long fly about to find a new mate or territory. One very flighty, or very sociable, tagged female from Gateshead (a bird that is) ended up visiting Wales, Cumbria, Scotland and the Chilterns but they tend to stay local. Seeing them back in our streets and in city skies does seem only right.

Saying that, it can be a shock as they fly into a small bird table for scraps in a suburban garden, almost scraping their wings on the fence as they do. But this is also an awe inspiring sight for children and their parents. A new generation of kite watchers is growing up around release sites.

They have found it hard to spread away from their comfort zones, so often you will see quite a few kites together in groups and they can look really spectacular. On one landfill site I watched, over thirty red kites roosted and foraged nearby. As the day darkened more and more of these great birds spiralled in and sat like bronzed statues of themselves in the branches of a dead sycamore. It felt and looked as if they were falling from the sky, as if from some invisible tunnel from the past, red kites as sky litter, gliding down to the Earth.

Their future is not guaranteed absolutely. They are still persecuted and poisoned, many killed annually, and some are even calling for a cull. The very prejudice that had made them so rare in the first place still remains in some quarters. One highly recognised individual bird, wing tagged and adopted by local schools in Riding Mill, was shot, and the community outrage and shame that came from it seems to have ensured it was a one off incident, locally. But over twenty were killed on one estate in Scotland in 2013. Perhaps they are at their safest in the City, as an accepted part of the local community.

I had the privilege of seeing one of the last Gateshead or 'northern kites' released from its rearing pen, near Gibside, one cold, damp morning a few years ago. It was a great feeling to see this cage-reared bird from Norway find its freedom and to see, at such close quarters, its beauty.

Red kites are stunning birds of prey. They may have the habits of a vulture but they are glamorous by comparison. As big as a buzzard, but with thinner more kinked wings, they have a mode of flight that is actually kite-like. They move and parry in the air and hover at times, glide and circle, dipping and rising on the updrafts. Their distinctive, deep cut V-shaped tail is a very flexible, fan-like extension, functioning as a rudder.

Close up, they have a serious expression but a blonde, shaggy, over the collar, cowl of head and neck feathers and their wing and back feathers really do live up to their name. They shine red and rusty in the sunlight.

In my mind's eye I will always think of kites first as Welsh and wild and not particularly 'Northumbrian' at all. I will always remember that excitement I felt, when I first glimpsed and recognised the V-shaped tail. A red kite floated above me as I picnicked with my parents, while on holiday near Aberystwyth. My later trips to the Welsh hills

were also formative.

But now I and others also get a different feeling, one of reassurance, mixed with a little amazement that this icon of conservation success has returned and is once more among us in urban Northumbria and looks so at home.

*(Allendale and Teesdale tops)*

# Famous Grouse

As with the whisky, as with the bird. The black grouse liquor is the darker side of the Famous Grouse brand. It is described as being more smoky and peaty than its red grouse stalwart, more full bodied, inspired as it is by the rarer species of heather bird and its more 'extroverted, feathered character'.

You can only take this whisky ornithological analogy so far but it works usefully and it is fun to taste the drams, rolling them around your mouth, whilst contemplating the particularities of bird and blend. After all, both whisky and bird are distillations, embodiments of their landscape and habitat and you might, as you mellow, also conclude, as it says on the box, that 'both whisky and conservation take commitment and time to produce great results'.

These marketing types know how to spin a good whisky yarn and a picture also helps. The black grouse illustrated on the supermarket shelf is a more muscular, polished, slick feathered beast than its tweedy red cousin. The red grouse reminds me of open, managed moors and shooting butts, the black grouse takes me to rarer places and corners of the landscape, where I need to look hard for a rare bird pushed to the edges with trickier habitat requirements.

We might take the red for granted, its wildness undermined by being pampered and 'farmed' as a game bird. But its darker relative is something we rarely see, a joy revealed when you catch up with it, the males exotic and jungle-fowl like in their display behaviour. The two grouse illustrate different sides to the character of our Northumbrian uplands.

Black grouse inhabit the rough, scrubby edges of the moors and bogs of the North Pennines and Northumberland. They like less tidy landscapes and hence they are more common in the Scottish moors and away from heavily managed grouse moors. They want tree cover, a place to roost and congregate, not too out in the open. Often they frequent wet flushes and rushy patches on the lip of the moor or a slope, not so much heather birds, as scrubby heath birds of the high montane. The label on Black Grouse whisky therefore shows it in rougher, higher terrain, the red, on a bright, managed heather moor.

Sometimes black grouse fly high. I have seen them from a distance in tree tops, looking like shredded bin-bags, caught amongst branches. Other times, in the winter, you may see them in numbers, congregating on the lower slopes of Pennine dales, as if just waiting for something to do.

Once ubiquitous, they are no longer common at all, even in north-west Northumbria, which is their last English outpost. Gone are the times when they, like the red grouse, were regarded as fair game and shot for the pot and fun, alongside snipe, woodcock, partridge and plover, though numbers are still shot in Scotland. I wonder how it tastes, tucking into such beautiful rarity?

The best way to see them is at their spring breeding sites, or leeks, the male's territorial stalking ground. Often these are stuck to for decades, sometimes becoming staked out, esoteric and little talked about, patches of rather strange human and bird behaviour.

Watching a lek feels voyeuristic. It is, after all, breaking in on the intimate, mating rituals of the black grouse. It involves observing closely a particular patch of ground in the middle of nowhere, creeping up and concealing yourself in the dark. This is done alone, or with close companions; yes, it has an odd feel, though most wildlife watching is like that.

It's just that the black grouse lek is all about passion. It is when the males, greatly inflamed and at their glossiest, black-plumed best, are plumped up to ward off rivals and display their dancing skills. There is something a little fetish-like about their garb and structured moves. The dominant, male blackcock takes over the middle of the rough circle and starts a lot of fast running about, puffing up and raising and lowering his sharp, black wings, which are white studded along their edge for effect. He makes strange, flowing neck movements, his cherry red eyebrows shine forth, as he raises his white tail into a shaking fan. All the way through, the males make a low vibrating, cooing sound.

You could, if you were so inclined, describe lek watching as a cross between a Northern Soul dance off and a Funky Chicken demo, in the context of a 'dogging' meeting!

Human antics aside, the grouse conduct themselves with grace and beauty; slow ,soft, stepping movements are punctuated by explosive displays of wings or kicks into the air, very much in the style of Chen Tai Chi, or vice versa. More often than not it is we that mimic Nature, not the other way around.

The conditions have to be right. Leks are at their best in warm, still weather, as the moon goes down and the sun comes up. It is an early morning man thing. They want atmosphere, a stage, an audience. That's where the female greyhens come in. Understated and visiting around the edges of the arena, they lie low and try to ignore the males' show off antics, but become part of the winner's harem quite naturally, when all is done and the victor struts his stuff, testosterone overflowing into frenzied mating.

Local advice and a reliable guide is essential to get the most from 'lekking'. The rarity of these birds and the privilege of watching them, when you can track them, is a real concern. The over manicured grouse moors in northern England and the extensive, upland planting of conifers do not favour them, in contrast to just over the border in Scotland and Cumbria, where more varied microhabitats persist and numbers are consequently higher.

Only in the far reaches of upper Teesdale and Weardale, the Allen Valley and perhaps the wooded edges of the Cheviots might you succeed. I have been lucky just a few times and I always hope, but usually fail, to make this an annual ritual of my own, seeing the black grouse lek, if only to remind me again of how fragile some of our Northumbrian wildlife is and how much it is still in need of care.

So, until that next time, I will just have to reach for the Famous Black Grouse and content myself with memories and hopes for the future. That deserves a toast. I propose, 'to the blackcock, may he lek another day!'

*(Dufton Pike, Roseberry Topping and Arthur's Seat)*

# *Marilyns*

'Hold on mate, there's Hong Kong Phooey up 'ere doing his thingy, don't startle him, he's close to the edge!'. I love practising Tai Chi on the tops of hills and mountains and Roseberry Topping is the closest to a mountain there is in the Cleveland Hills.

So there I am, getting into my stride, when, the first of fifteen walkers join me on the top of Teesside, to admire the view and moan about, 'that bloodyill'. I carry on, they move away, tranquillity is restored. Not just peace and quiet, but a sense of being somewhere very special, a high point in every sense, a great energy of place. Here, on the most outstanding of the Cleveland Hills, I turn and twist, float and soar in the breeze, a 21st Century 'shaman' in his element, I like to think.

I was off dreaming again, but this was, after all, the local 'sacred mountain' even in Viking times known as Odin's Hill. According to archaeologists, great, geological outliers like this and also the rounded hills of Freeborough and Gold Hill nearby, were perhaps as sacred in their time as the Himalayan Kenchunjenga and Kylash still are. Up here, people took what Nature offered and enhanced it to satisfy their ritual needs.

It was a minimalist approach, not the bale and bluster of Stonehenge and Avebury, where, in the form of the conical Silbury, they had to make their own hill. Here the landscape readily provided the shapes of sanctity. The same can be said of other sacred, ancient hills like Simonside and Yeavering in Northumberland. We made the best of our natural assets up North.

Roseberry has a place in the minds and memories of all around here.

103

It is still a significant hill. Many books have featured it and in 2000 the local community published a comprehensive study of its place in people's lives. In other words it is still revered.

For me and others, it carries memories of hard days' walks as a kid, of rolling eggs and picking bluebells, crying in the heat of the bracken, or kissing too, in later years.

Its shape led to its nickname of the 'Cleveland Volcano', though it is not the remains of a volcanic plug, but an upstanding chunk of hard sandstone. It has, however, an igneous element, the Cleveland Dyke, a vertical incision of cooled and metamorphosed magma running up its side, quarried into a linear cutting for road stone.

As budding, student geologists, we were encouraged to explore the linear quarry running up to its flank. The quarry sides showed the effects of superheated rock injection, metamorphosing sedimentary layers into shiny schists, with garnets and other minerals. Higher up, we found fossilised ferns in the once deltaic sandstones, just under the summit. All the history of the Earth was accessible on one medium-sized hill.

As much as anything, Roseberry and the Cleveland Hills are an escape from the busyness and smog of downtown Teesside. They offer a taste of Nature on the doorstep and have been revered as such for years. They are also appreciated by long distance walkers 'doing' the Cleveland Way or Coast to Coast.

I look on these as modern-day, landscape pilgrims, eating up the land as they go, in their target driven efforts to cover the miles, day after day. No doubt, whether they are looking for it or not, some of the tranquillity, even the sanctity, of their wild Nature, rubs off on them.

These and other smaller local hills across Northumbria provide us with a taste of the mountains. For most of us there is often not the time or energy to climb a mountain, but you still want to get off the ground, well above yourself, to be among clouds, free your mind in space and beauty.

This is when you need a 'Marilyn', as opposed to a Munro (a mountain over 3000 feet). A Marilyn is a small but perfectly formed hill, around 500 feet in height, that might be scaled in an hour or two or even less, but which gives you the sense of a climb and the challenge of steep, rugged terrain, a mountain in miniature. Roseberry is certainly that.

Arthur's Seat, in Edinburgh is a great example, a good place to clear the head after a few days of over indulgence at the Festival. This is a true volcanic plug and one of the classic sites for early geologists. Unfortunately for me, it is associated more with hangovers and rain!

My absolute favourite Marilyn anywhere is Dun I on Iona, a little hill with a lot of charisma and punching far above its size in terms of its effect. Twenty minutes up hill and you come panting to one of the best views on Earth. Views are often the very reason to climb, but there is also, on even a small climb, an ascension into wildness and these small hills propel you from the ground to highness in one short, sharp burst.

I seem attracted by pointed, volcano-like, largish hills just as I was drawn to the shape of that true and challenging mountain in the west of Scotland that inspired my quest, to risk my life to climb it, on the off chance; for me, there is a compulsion to climb.

Dufton Pike is one such place. One of several, distinctly conical peaks you pass as you traverse the A66 between Scotch Corner and Penrith, on the edge of the Pennines. On the way back from a meeting and having driven, it seems, through and past the whole of the landscapes of the north in just a few days without actually setting foot in them, I choose Dufton as the place to physically reacquaint

105

myself. Sometimes looking is not enough, you have to get up there. There is a lot to be said for spontaneity.

After getting lost a few times in the back lanes, I find the red sandstone village of Dufton and discover the paths to the Pike are actually formed of a bifurcation of the Pennine Way. If I had more time and inclination I would strike out onto the top of the Pennines, over to Cross Fell but that is for another day. It is a short fix of hill I need.

I have to walk up to the foot of Dufton Pike for about a mile or so, but it is instantly beautiful and charming, following hollow ways between bare and twisting ash trees, crossing bubbling streams between drystone walls, real Pennine country, a taste of the limestone hills.

Gradually I make my way upwards, through pasture and thorn scrub, to the western tail of the long whaleback, ending in a flat cone, which forms Dufton Pike. It is a hard pull up, very steep and I go off-piste hacking through thick grass, stopping now and then to watch the crows who seem to be keeping an eye on me.

It is getting interesting; the wind is strong all the way up and raw, but as I climb there is a sense of getting among and into the high lands. To the north I look onto the plateau of the Pennines and note the presence of snow, even in late March, in what has been a snowless winter, or so I thought. These foothills of volcanic plugs eroded by weather and time are now partly grass covered cones, and offer hill top viewpoints into the rougher moors above and beyond, the cold Pennine interior.

The sun shines on me as I 'summit' Dufton, but looking out over the nearby Pennine ridge there is no sunlight at all, just grey, billowing cloud and an icy wind coming off the tops, the fragments of snow, black heathered moors and mires, looking as if the glaciers have just retreated. I have the sense of standing on the threshold between two worlds.

From the Pike top I stare down into High Cup Nick and its little waterfall and path, a natural gateway into the Pennines and I picture the first settlers of these parts who followed a wild larder on the hoof and probably donned skins and furs as basic protection against an uncompromising land. Today, it looks as if it hasn't changed much at all.

In fact I am glad to be sitting on my lesser hill in what feels like a gale force wind, as it is nowhere near as bleak as the picture before me. In relative comfort I am afforded high elevation and insight. I have no need to venture further, I am uplifted enough.

I run down the other side and dawdle between walls back to the village, noting the early nest building antics of a pair of grey wagtails, under a bridge that looks carved from the rocks around. They remind me it is actually now early spring. There are signs of leaves on the hedges, primroses, violets and celandines opening. But glimpsing back, up to the Pennine massif, spring has not sprung there yet. It is still stuck in the Ice Age.

This escape to the hills lasted for just over two hours. I feel rejuvenated, time stretched itself. Indeed I feel as though I have somehow travelled back in time, glimpsed an icy past. As ever, I am reminded small hills hold strong medicine.

*To the **Guts** of it all, experiencing the diversity of the middle-land, Yorkshire and the Tees Valley*

## Yorkshire–Lands

Tees Valley and North Yorkshire are my home patch, the ecosystem I grew up in. Elements of wildness spread out like green fingers, from the smoggy sprawl of the Tees estuary, bleeding out into the purer countryside of the North York Moors and East Cleveland, down to Whitby and Scarborough and onto the chalk lands of the Humber-Wolds. Eventually these meet up with and blend into the southern Yorkshire and South Pennine moors and the Dales.

This is an enormous swathe of land of different landscapes and local cultures. Yorkshire has a strong identity, with a sense of a York-centred culture, going back to the Romans and Vikings. Yet there is also a prevailing feeling of belonging and shared history with the North East, a Northumbrian kinship.

What is obvious, by now, is that we belong to landscapes, natural areas, as much as we do to contrived counties. Likewise, the wildlife and wild places reflect the distinctiveness of locality and habitat type, the opportunities presented to them by our urban and industrial development and the rural places we manage in various ways.

There is a reassuring familiarity between Yorkshire, Northumberland and Pennine, moors, bogs and other big landscape types, as well as interesting local differences to explore. Overall Yorkshire is more populous, less wild and yet there are many wild places and echoes.

As well as the similarity with environs further north, similar prehistoric remains are found and there are Celtic Christian outposts aplenty in the many abbeys, churches and monasteries, in key locations which tell, again, of the Celtic spirit of place and association with Nature.

To me, this is an intimate land, a place of lifelong memory and experience, where land and life merge into an inspiring tapestry, historically rooted, but very much part of a modern Northumbria.

*(Northumberland Hills, Danby moors,
Haworth and Ilkley)*

## Merlin Moors

"What was that?!" A small, dark, scythe-shaped missile whizzes across the moor, chasing an even smaller brown bird which drops suddenly into the heather. The missile flings out a claw, raising dust from the pipit's wing. This one got away.

The 'trident' comes to rest on a rock amongst deep, purple heather. It is instantly recognisable now as the smallest and one of the fiercest and fastest of our birds of prey, the merlin, denizen of Northumbrian moors.

So associated with remote and wild moorland is the merlin that they utterly embody it. Just as Emily Bronte's Heathcliff, of Wuthering Heights, was described as being 'an arid wilderness of furze and whinstone', so too is the bird. Its whole demeanour is an extension of its rough home. No other bird sums up the moorland environment so well, apart from the red grouse, it's more sedate, heather ingesting, neighbour. The fearless, impish merlin captures the sometimes malevolent mood of the moors.

They inhabit the corners and shoulders of remotest moorland, hiding and hunting in their contours, favouring the edges and horizons, the frame of the landscape: shifting shadows, moving over moor and mire, flush, flash, hag and bog.

They nest and rest in canopied hollows, where the leggiest heather overtops itself and cascades down slopes. Only those who have marked them for years, monitoring them for ornithological or other reasons, know where to find them.

Everything about them is wild. Their plumage mimics the coarse weft and warp of their habitat, the brown barred tweed of the female, the dark grey-blue, flecked suit of the male, his breast tinged with russet as if bits of the red-brown bog asphodel were picked up and woven into it. They blend in. Even their shining, black eyes reflect the scenery as they look through you.

My encounters with the merlin range from seeing them up close and personal on the North York Moors, to the high moor of Kielder and glimpses of their 'battarang' shapes, ghosting across the Bronte moors near Haworth.

At the atmospheric, old parsonage, where the Brontes lived, wrote and died so young, I discovered that Emily Bronte kept a pet merlin she had rescued. 'Nero' lived for some years, was kept in a cage and taken out to be painted and drawn. He became an inspiration and pertinent reminder of the tamed fury Emily captured in her hand and prose.

The merlin, then, is one way of coming to terms with the essence of the moors, which so dominate our northern uplands. If you are from Yorkshire or Northumberland or Pennine country, the moor is not just a place, but a cultural construct.

They seep into your psyche. In the same way you can be immersed in forest or fen. People can take on some of their rugged form and changeable moods, welcoming and off-putting, by turns. We are subliminally aware of their associations, Heathcliff and Wuthering Heights, Hounds of the Baskervilles, moor murders. They have their own, literary canon and mythology.

We were never programmed to like moorland. It is an unnatural association, their character merely a result of Bronze Age man's deforestation, an environmental catastrophe. But we have grown to love them.

It is the mix of their openness and seeming naturalness. Their habitat mosaics feel wild but we even like that they are inhospitable. Experiencing them is so weather-driven. In their vast hill top exposure, they hold and play with cloud and light, changing in seconds. Like mountains, they offer an endless canvas onto which we can project our thoughts and very being. Seeing these heather seas disappear into the horizon, we are drawn to look into our minute selves.

Each moor is slightly different: from the endless wilderness of the Scottish borders and Pennines (sometimes over managed for grouse) to the more intimate vignettes of Haworth, Ilkley and little outliers like Eston Moor, on the back of the scarp, looming above Teesside's industry.

Three of many moorland memories, in three seasons, underline their different effects.

*- Urra Moor, Winter*

Into the white I climb, drawn upwards by shining snow, icing the top of Urra Moor. The reflected light feels blinding. Coincidentally, a man passes me as I slide along and we exchange a few words, 'A few weeks back I had to stop the hill race I was in, I was off work for days, with snow blindness.' Snow, sunlight, it can happen, even here, in North Yorkshire.

The journey up feels formidably steep, but the weather is so bright it is like an engine on my back, firing me onwards. I follow the well-marked path through melting snow, around the edge of a stone wall that exactly traces the shape of the hill, to the very point that ends in a stone tongue, sticking out in mid- air.

Here I rest awhile on what locals call the 'Cheese Stone'. Like a stone altar, it hangs over Bilsdale with its big, hollowed-out basin, gouged cup marks and channels, where melting snow gathers and spills, ending in a thin cascade over the rock face, glinting in the sun. It is the sort of place to anoint yourself.

A sudden movement to my right has me skidding to a few isolated rocks, where I catch sight of the black tip of a stoat's tail and the spiral tracks of its feet, snow dust sprinkling from the little cave it has entered.

But I am dawdling, putting off the long ascent towards thicker snow, pushing my arthritic hip pain inside. I am up here proving to myself I can do it. Once I start, it is wonderful, real snow, calf deep. Gradually, the landscape envelops me. My small, dark shape moves slow and deliberate in a totally white land, only the dark lines of paths and the odd standing stone visible. One, a big heart of a rock, I use as a shield to rest by.

The Round Hill on top of Urra has its own white obelisk, a trig point, and is a natural viewpoint. In the distance you can make out the Wainstones, a landmark line-up of ancient ritual significance. This day it looks frozen in white, photographic. Nothing moves.

Then, from between my feet, there is a tiny flurry. With an energy far exceeding its size, a pygmy shrew is whirling around on the snow, a tiny dervish, spiralling over my coat and bag and diving into a small tunnel at the foot of the trig point, emerging again to skitter under the crusty snow. It weaves between tiny, ice-sculpture forests in the frozen heather, just a blur, before coming up and bouncing away, out of sight.

It is a surreal moment, one of those times you think, it was either serendipity, or something meant to be: coincidence or synergy. It also feels symbolic of survival against the odds, how vulnerable and resilient life can be.

It seems to re-energise me enough to face the return. It is very cold now and getting dark. I feel 'semi- freddo', my legs as heavy as a yeti's. I shuffle back down the snow-shrouded moor, content that I've made it, the glare from the snow lighting my way

### - *Commondale Moor, Summer*

I recall a day of fire and heat walking upon Commondale Moor. It is like walking on dry tinder, as if it might burst into combustion at any moment. In the late afternoon I approach the top of the moors, moving towards an intriguing line of stones which start or end at a cluster of Bronze Age barrows, the Black Howes, sweltering in the heat. It's like being in an upland desert.

I watch a couple of stonechats, their bright pink and ochre throats look as if they have been singed. I walk over square-cut carpets of black moor, burnt purposefully to encourage new heather for grazing grouse. A golden plover mournfully pleads to me with its cat-like mewing, to 'go back, go back' until I almost do seek cool streams.

Instead, blinking towards the lines of standing stones, silhouetted in the high sun, I trace the ridge from rush-filled hassock to hill. Then dark clouds muster around the sun for a few moments, giving some relief from the scorching heat and hinting at the possibility of thunder and rain. But no, the cloud sidles off, leaving just a stain of peat hagg on the sky.

This is a day to infuse the heat and scent of moor, its tinctures of whisky essences, and a cocktail of musky acidity. You relax and feel warmed through, daydreaming about the meaning of a line of old stones, a ditch and bank, the burial mound with a stone at its centre, all the people who passed this way in rain, snow and sun.

It is the thought of beer, inevitably, that gets me out of my dream state and back down the hill where, browned and blackened, I discover that I too, have been burnished, by the moor.

*- Ilkley Moor, Autumn*

Every moor has an ever evolving story to tell. If moors can be clichés, Ilkley Moor is just that. Immortalised in song and satirised by all who think they can exaggerate a Yorkshire accent, it is the quintessential Yorkshire Moor: 'Ilkley Moor ba'tat'. I avoided it as a consequence.

When I did eventually visit, I was the only person singing the ear-worming song, under my breath and I found its moorland magic. This is centred on its geo-archaeological features, gritstone outcrops, shaped by weather and inscribed and placed by man over millennia, all melting, one feature into the next, so that the human and the natural become one.

This is the way into understanding this moor, contained all around by visible ridges, beyond which the land falls steeply away to valley. There are over four hundred rock art features, nearly all named, along with hundreds more, natural outcrops, given names too, reflecting their forms. This is another Northumbrian place where early man ritualised an animated landscape and described it in a mysterious, symbolic language.

Saying their names aloud brings the place to life: the Cow and Calf: the Swastika Rock: the Badger Stone: the Doubler Rocks: Cloven Rock: West Buck Rock: the Kirkstones: the Thimble Stones: Todmoor Stone: the Two Eggs: Ilkley Crags: the Great Skirtfull of Stones: Wetstone Gate: the Millstones: the Twelve Apostles stone circle: Little Skirtfull of Stones: the Pancake Stone: Rocky Valley: West Rock: White Crag: Wicken Tree Crag: Backstone Beck… and so on.

Of these, the Cow and Calf rocks are hulking outcrops, which tower over the town. The Calf's giant boulder looks stopped mid spin, on the down slope, waiting for the chocks to be removed so it can continue its crushing journey. Close inspection of the Cow and the other crags reveal they have been carved with names and symbols, from prehistoric to modern times, with some forthright 18th Century and Victorian examples. These are marks of proclamation, affection and association, tombstone records of the living.

On top of this, there are recent additions. 'The Stanza Stones', poetry etched and placed amongst the rocks here, the work of Simon Armitage and Ilkley Literature Festival. They carry on the tradition of using words to encode the changing moods of place.

We go one day to discover 'the Puddlestone' and find it laid on its back between natural cubes of grit they call the Thimble Stones. The poem tells of great, dark clouds like horses, clattering their way across hills and dropping their 'rain junk' out of black skies. It perfectly describes our day.

Likewise, after we miss, then find, 'the Beckstone' in Backstone Beck and its poem, which imagines the waters of the moors starting from a tear in a curlew's eye, we see the birds later, near 'the Badger Stone'. It is as if the poems are real reflections, portents, of the landscape we are experiencing.

Pausing this one last time, we pour the remains of our water bottles onto a wedge of carved boulder. We watch as rivulets flow and highlight its cup and ring marks and carved gullies, just as it finally starts to rain. It looks as if it is crying.

It seems at every level, on every rock, the landscape and people are speaking to us. Ilkley is a moor that sings its own song.

These are the moorlands then, the backbone of upland Northumbria. They are to be experienced singly, or as one entity, if you can face the 268 mile Pennine Way and even then you will not touch them all. But however you meet them, they exude an undeniable power of place. Over thousands of years of cohabitation with its peoples, a relationship has been forged that is as varied as it is contradictory.

Thus, I have not decided yet I think, if I 'like' moors, as places; they are not my chosen habitat. But I know they are part of me and I am thankful for their space fullness and sense of wild, the tales they tell and the feelings they evoke.

*(Tees Flyover and Saltholme,
Tees estuary, Greatham Creek)*

# Flyover

*Little Egret – Saltholme
9.45 21.10.10*

I'm distracted on my way to work, tearing up the A19 just south of the Tees flyover, by what look like two little egrets in a tree. They are just off the side of the old meander of the River Tees, which runs between two sides of an industrial estate. I have to check this out and stop on the hard shoulder. They are two egrets alright, as white and clean as two, new washing machines.

These two birdy 'white goods' are incongruously perched in a large hawthorn on the back of the tidal river, next to a chain link fence guarding a brick wall. They are pure white, middle-sized herons, with bright yellow eyes and, close up, greenish legs with a central, dark stripe down their toes, a sort of eyebrow pencil stocking seam. They carry a lacy head plume, slinking over the back of their heads which bobs as they move, the targets for ladies' hats in Victorian times.

Later that same day, I watch half a dozen of their brethren on the River Wansbeck, at Castle Island, stalking the muddy shores. They are eeling with their serpent-like necks and javelin bills, looking every inch the feathered saurian. Their staccato movement, gently flowing through the waters and then flicking open their wings like fans, remind me of the African black heron which creates an umbrella effect with mantled wings, invoking sudden shade to attract small fish to its feet.

I always associate egrets with the Hayle and Fal estuaries in Cornwall which is where they first started to breed and colonise England in the 1990s. They have since spread northwards and are today one of the most recent additions to the Northumbria breeding bird list, nesting for the first time in Northumberland at Druridge Pools in 2014. They always seem exotic.

In this same lovely summer, spoonbills, glossy ibis and a great white heron, were also seen in the area, giving a distinctively Mediterranean feel to the North. The egret's advance is an expansion of its range as the climate warms year on year.

This Teesside pair's purity and elegance seem so out of kilter with their dirty, dilapidated surroundings. I had seen cormorants, gulls and the odd heron here before, but never egrets. Then I am often taken aback by the wildlife I see among the industrial landscape of the Tees.

I set off before the egret police catch up with me and head over the great arch of concrete, affording a brief overview of the industrial heart of Teesside. As I do so I am again surprised, this time to see a great spotted woodpecker, its red and pied plumage catching in the bright light, against a backdrop of chemical plants and the trees of Riverside Park, formerly the Ironmasters site, which was filled, in the 19th Century with over 20 ironworks.

Sidling along in heavy traffic, I notice the glinting wetlands to my left at Portrack Marsh, a nature reserve on the bank of the river next to a sewage farm and near the Tees Barrage. This is an industrial wildlife oasis, true marsh and reed bed wildness amongst the grime.

Unlikely as it may seem, otters frequent its pools and they use the metal criss-crossed pipe bridges of industry to take short cuts across the waterways. I have actually seen a big dog otter come up on the bank with a sea trout in its mouth that a seal had killed and let go. The barrage is a congregating place for grey seals chasing migratory fish dinners.

The ultimate expression of the biodiversity of the industrial Tees is no doubt Saltholme nature reserve near Port Clarence on the North Tees estuary. This area has always been great for birding: pools left over from industry, wet fields and marshes. The creeks and saltmarshes of the estuarine edges and the estuary mudflats of Bran Sands make it a very special place. I well recall childhood jaunts here to see birds like ruff, waders whose males acquire unique and gaudy head dresses in Summer, the 'Lady Boys' of the bird world. There were winter flocks of wildfowl and waders and a raft of seasonal, vagrant rarities.

Today Saltholme brings this all together into one, linked landscape mosaic with an impressive visitor centre and new hides and extended habitats. The industrial backdrop and almost bleak setting is mercurial, especially at dawn or sunset. There is always much to see, not just birds. I have had great close up views of foxes, stoats and hares here too.

In some ways, the reserve and its many conservation partners have formalised what was there unofficially, surviving unnoticed or tolerated, occasionally celebrated. The industrial green corridors and protected green space within factory fences were always rewarding.

Years ago I visited one where the night shift regularly fed over twenty foxes. Owls too were often seen; short eared, long eared (there is a winter roost site of them at Saltholme, amazing to see) and barn owl all live here.

With the new development have come improved management and more eyes watching and therefore even more rarities and surprises recorded. It is good to see the avocet, an ornithological symbol of hope and recovery against all odds, now breeding. And it is always good to see an egret.

Saltholme might have been called, 'Serendipity', as you never really know what to expect. One of the most beautiful birds I have seen there, totally on the off chance, was a passerine white-winged black tern. It was pure bird eye-candy, a refined, white, small gull-like tern with a floating, hovering, butterfly flight and two-tone wings, as if it was flashing its satin lined jacket as it flew towards us. Off course, it should have been in the Balkans.

Perhaps the most disappointing, by contrast, was a bewildered looking, small grey finch, in a bush, all the way from Russia. Its thick, pencil-lead bill made it look solemn and accentuated its appearance of bewilderment. It was the exotically named, scarlet rosefinch but this one had lost its scarlet rose.

More than anything, North Tees is a place to get close to Nature in the most unnatural setting you could find. Approach it from the Boro side, across the Transporter Bridge by cycle for the whole experience and look up and wonder at the tales of prostitutes, plying their trade on the sky high gantry above, as workers came home from work, which must surely be an urban myth.

You'd have to be a peregrine to do it up there! But then, we should never be surprised at what we find, amongst the industry of the Tees.

*(Guisborough Moor
and Sleddale)*

# Rough Legged Sleddale

Sleddale is another hidden pearl of Northumbria, this time locked into the 'in-by lands', those improved grazing strips that come right up to the moor edge in the North York Moors. These lands may well have been cleared in the Iron Age or even earlier, mini Alps for late summer grazing of the first farmed sheep. They are the favoured nesting haunts and feeding areas for birds such as peewit and golden plover, green islands in a sea of heather.

In big sweeping open u-shaped dales such as Farndale in the middle of the Moors, these in-byes head up substantial fields coming right up the sides of the valley, but they are considerably less lush and productive in the narrower, steeper-sided ones like Westerdale and Commondale.

Sleddale is hardly a dale at all, being no more than a tiny valley squeezed between the arms of Guisborough Moor and almost hidden from view until you are upon it. As well as its small scale neatness, it holds an occasional ornithological high for which it is famed in birding circles.

It may be approached from several directions but there are two I favour. From the village of Commondale you can go up and over Skelderskew Moor and past its intriguing line of megaliths and clusters of Bronze Age barrows at Hob on the Hill and Black Howes, onto the back of Guisborough Moor. Or you can start at Hutton village on the edge of Guisborough Forest and come up and over the moor to the little dale.

This time I visit purposely in the dead of winter, with a sprinkling of snow and the ground tight with frost. I am looking for a winter uplift.

I walk up through Hutton, itself a place of medieval wood pasture and parkland, fizzling into the conifer plantations of the forest. This has some lovely, old 'doddery' ash and oaks with hollow centres, great for beetles and birds. Until recent times this was one of the few reliable places in the North East you could bet on seeing the lesser spotted woodpecker but the range and numbers of these sparrow-sized peckers have vastly contracted now and it is rarely seen, even in the south west, where they feel at home. Now and then they are picked up at places like Potteric Carr, near Doncaster.

The mere memory of them excites. I have encountered them in the ancient woods of the Wye Valley and nesting in ruined, stately parkland in Birmingham. I fondly remember watching two birds displaying to one another, with their bizarre wing lifting and shaking moves, as if revving themselves up before launching into florid butterfly flights, two black and white shuttlecocks dipping and diving in the early morning mist of a woodland clearing, surrounded by equally rare, wild service trees.

Back in Hutton, I climb quickly up to the crag that is visible from everywhere around Guisborough, Highcliff, the look up to and a look out from place.

From here I strike out past a couple of prominent, stone cairns, ridge top burial sites, and face a freezing, ferocious wind. I am forced downhill early to take shelter in Sleddale. It is the only chance of any solace from the wind and cold. I stumble through heather, having lost any sense of path and almost fall upon a couple of big outcrops, against which I stop to get my breath.

Here I take in the little dale just below. It is a perfect, long rectangle, a tablecloth of green spread on the floor of a flat-bottomed mini valley where, in neat fields, flocks of sheep graze, undisturbed. Down the valley you can see the little, white farmhouse of Percy Rigg, from which point the whole merges back in with the receding headlands and moors beyond, horizon after horizon, disappearing into the diaphanous haze.

I wander down and take in the sense of calm and cultivated control of the dale in miniature, then scramble over a fast flowing beck and sit in the heather, looking back over the dale, feeling utterly wind and cold blasted. I'm ready for home and wondering why I bothered to choose today to search for birds.

Then it appears, the reason I came here: a large bird of prey, silhouetted in the sky, above the far ridge. It is flapping its strong wings and hovering like an out of scale kestrel, its shape and habits unmistakeable. Gradually, the bird swoops, fighting the wind and hunting, close to the ground, chasing rabbits. Once or twice it even lands on the ground and I have superb views as it banks slowly and circles maybe a hundred metres from where I sit.

It is a rough legged buzzard: a bigger, whiter, longer-tailed version of the common buzzard and a rare winter migrant from Norway. For some reason, a pair or two find their way to the North York Moors every winter and are often seen in this area.

They are thrilling birds to see, powerful yet graceful harriers and hoverers. Once, on my birthday in November, we stayed in Commondale and had a roadside close-up of one. It looked like an osprey with its under-wings of black and white patchwork and cream, over the collar, feathered head-dress. What a bird. Its grandeur was enhanced by its appearance in this tiny, tidy valley.

As today's bird finally glides out of sight, I too steal away and run all the way back to the car, the spirit of this eagle-like bird's energy propelling me all the way.

*(Boulby alum
quarries)*

# Quarry Owls

They're crafty these little owls, gone to ground today in sea fret, all of their usual perching points deserted. I check each in turn anyway, marked by their chalk mark excretions. Most of the bigger, angular, sandstone boulders, in the old alum quarry above the sea, bear their stripes. The owls love it here, except in this weather. It's a cold evening of fret in April with a wet Bank Holiday feel to it. Wisely, they are holed up.

At least one is hunkered down on the nest. On better days I've seen them flying in and out of the bole of an old willow, rooted deep under the jumbled, quarried blocks. Close up, you can just make out the nursery in the hollow willow basket, hidden within its flailing branches.

Last year they chose a burrow nest on a quarry ledge, where they pushed up the turf like a rug and tunnelled under it. Their comings and goings were comical, having to bend down to enter or leave, exploding, face-first out of their dark barrel home without warning. I swore then that these birds had to be the inspiration for tales of hobbits and gnomes.

Often the male bird stands on sentry duty on a boulder nearby, still, and with eyelids dropping. There is apparent affection between the pair, when they alight at the nest together or when he greets her as she emerges. They sit and shoulder shimmy next to one another, occasionally touching beaks in a form of Maori kiss. Other times they will fly over one another calling out. Not today. Maybe they're both in there keeping warm?

Anyhow, I miss their winning ways, which bring the place alive with owl energy. Small they may be in stature but not in character. I have watched them and their eccentric habits for years. They seem so much part of this place and the countryside generally, wherever they pop up.

I have to remind myself that they are not native to these isles, having been introduced only a hundred years before I was born from southern Europe. They are the national bird of Greece, so they are not part of the ancient make-up but the recent, natural history of Northumbria. Despite this, they seem to have found a niche that causes no problems for native birds, with the odd exception.

Unlike bigger British owls these sprites do not major on mice and other furry, fast food. Invertebrates are favoured, beetles and worms largely. But they have also developed special tactics for wren hunting.

It is a waiting game. They follow, almost nonchalantly, the rattling wrens around the quarry floor, hopping, seemingly haphazardly, from stone to rock. It turns out to be a stealthy posturing and positioning game and when the hapless wren appears within reach, it is grabbed by beak and talon and quickly consumed. It is quite a disturbing sight, the beautiful brown finery of the garden familiar being grabbed, stabbed and swallowed down!

They are, as are all owls, terribly territorial. They mark their boundaries by their constant calling, the repetitive 'creaking gate' some find irritating, uttered as they bob up and down, a pumping action to project their voices to maximum effect.

Their body language is a particularly endearing aspect of the little owl. They are shape shifters, elongating into elegance or compressing into rounded ovals, according to mood and circumstance. When active they look disturbed, manic. They pull themselves up, bobbing and weaving, moving from side to side to get the best view of danger or their prey, ever curious, with their lemon-yellow, penetrating eyes. At rest they are but brown-streaked blobs with slit eyes, on shut down, inwardly and outwardly contained, looking like chocolate Easter egg facsimiles.

This cold evening, if not in the nest, they are taking refuge under a snug rock ledge or warted onto a branch, invisible in the leaves, snuggling down with feathers fluffed out, full of worms and maybe even a wren or two, conserving their energy. These artful dodgers will wait it out till morning, let the weather break, then steal the show all over again.

When they are active, they are full of cheek, chasing up beetles from under cow pats in the fields, dangling worms from their bills as they stare at you from gate posts, challenging all comers with their glare. They are pretty lithe and long legged too, not as dumpy as they may look at rest. Their long 'kick-boxing' legs dangle as they fly or poke out sideways, from a sitting position, to catch passing prey.

A few years back the little owls were joined in their quarry by a pair of barn owls, unusually nesting on the cliff face. I expected trouble, assuming the quarry was not big enough for the both of them. In fact they carried on with their own business, occasionally screeching warnings to one another to keep their distance.

It made for great owl watching. Night after night my neighbour and birding companion Rocky and I could just about guarantee close-up views of the two species. Afterwards we referred to it as the 'Owl Summer' and still reflect on how lucky we were and so far it has not been repeated.

The barn owls bred in a deep slit of a recess in the sandstone cliff. As soon as they were mobile, the three chicks would shuffle to the edge and lookout, standing in a row like three puppet owls. From a distance we could watch their every move, sleeping, squabbling and preening themselves and each other, all the time uttering a wheezing purr that could be heard some way off. The industrious parents would glide in over the cliff edge, from the fields, clutching their prey of mice and voles, artfully turning in mid-air before entering the nest hole.

Later we would hold our breaths as the almost fully grown youngsters, still covered in fluffy down, became adventurous and tumbled down the cliff before pulling themselves back up onto ledges and tussocks. We even saw their whirring attempts at first flight, splattering with wings stretched out onto the grass and rocks below. Eventually, we had the privilege of seeing them fledge and take their first proper flights, confidently flying about the quarry from boulder to boulder, exploring their new world.

We watched them throughout the whole of the three months they bred there. We would see the adult birds covering their territory for prey, pushing the bounds of the fields and hedges, lanes and cliff tops, to feed themselves and their young, on average returning every fifteen minutes with a meal.

Often they would appear from the mist, carrying their prey and flying straight towards us, or hover over the cliff edge and shriek at us to move away. It felt, that summer, as if the cliffs and fields around Upton had become owned by the owls, day and night. Everywhere they would appear, as if haunting every last corner of their aerial zone.

They haunt me too; there is something prepossessing about their penetrating eyes. They have become my talisman birds, symbolising the wild, free qualities in Nature. Owls have been a part of the make-up of Northumbria from prehistoric times. Their ancestor, in the form of the bones of an Iron Age owl, was unearthed in an archaeological dig, in the very field the quarry owls fly over.

Over the years owls have acquired much mythology. They are the wise ones, the good luck or bad luck omens, flying reincarnations of lost souls. They occur today in all the special places that make Northumbria what it is, marking the wild side of the old Kingdom.

*(The Cleveland Hills and moors)*

# To The Wainstones

I am determined to climb up to the Wainstones, my favourite and oft visited point on the Cleveland Hills. These dramatic, ice-carved pinnacles that can be seen from miles away have charisma. The moors and rocks around are vibrant with life, past and present. It is a place I escape to in all conditions, just a mile long ridge walk, after scaling a steep ascent from the car park at Clay Bank, near Great Broughton. It is the place I headed for as soon as I recovered from hip surgery, a place of re-connection with self and Earth.

Today I kid myself I'm looking for 'fogbows', those curious weather effects caused by the reflection of sun or moon through mist or cloud, or glancing light off snow. On days like this the tops of hills are silenced by the mist. All they normally represent is enshrined within their thin cloak of white-out drizzle. Its real 'Yorkshire fog' this, like the grass here, of the same name, holding onto its droplets. No wind, after days of storms, makes it feel like the world has stopped spinning, gone into itself, an Earth meditation.

There are no fogbows today. Rather, I am dissolved into a silhouette and distilled into this ridge of land between Hasty Bank and the Wainstones outcrop. I can see in no direction, ambling towards 'the stones'.

Several times I steal off the path and sit shrouded for minutes, taking in the silence. Yes, there are sounds, but they are distant and muffled: a few cars on a road, a barking dog. They are a world away. The locked-in sounds around me are of grouse warbling, a pheasant calling suddenly, my breathing and the no voice of a delicate breeze, just teasing up the murmur of grass and the 'scritch scratch' of heather.

In this quietude I feel cut off from the trudge of human activity. Like slow falling snow, suspended in the air, the fog blankets and softens, bringing down a hush and we few walkers that are out up here today, presuming there are others, are suspended too. We are cloud dwellers, but with both feet on the ground.

Off piste, I follow a thin path through heather to a vague outline of a big rock, maybe fifty metres away to my left. I'm unsure, as even distance is muted. Whilst I know this place well, everything seems different; I've never been this way and never seen this rock before.

Its shape is revealed as I approach, a giant slab set against another and it is shaped so obviously into the head of a bird. I think 'crow', then 'raven'. It has a large bulbous 'bill' eight feet long, four wide. The rock even has a mark that implies a squinting eye. Someone has enhanced what appears to be a natural, sculptural accident by chiselling in a set of teeth on what to me is a lower mandible. They have made it into a monster. I see it differently.

I stumble back onto the main path and find a more familiar touchstone, a single boulder consciously carved with a heartfelt message: 'Christine, I love you', it proclaims. It has been there some years and is still pretty sharp and I always wonder how many women pass by and ask themselves if their partner would make such a permanent gesture, raw emotion, carved into the stones for all to see. As some of the other rock carvings about here show, this love note could endure a very long time.

Later, as the fog lifts for a short while, it reveals the full extent of the Wainstones themselves. I am just along the ridge from them, closer than I had thought. I clamber down, looking up and along them. As ever they are exquisite, naturally-sculpted, rocky outcrops. I walk past the long, tall shard of a pinnacle I call the 'Picasso stone' because its top is angled and bladed, like a Picasso abstract face or African mask. It also looks like a gigantic billhook suspended on high, ready to strike. Its shape has been chiselled by ice, wind and frost at the end of the Ice Age and it has stood there probably unchanged since.

The other parts of the sandstone have acquired names over the years and today, with the effect of the circling mists, these seem to ring more true than usual. I can clearly discern 'the sphinx', 'the monkey', 'the hatchet', 'the eagle' and 'the steeple'.

This is a well-loved spot and frequented by walkers, picnickers and climbers and it interests me how people are still drawn to its peculiar formation, as they have been perhaps since it was formed, thousands of years ago, as in so many of the special places of Northumbria. The Wainstones were once sacred stones, evidence of which lies below them, but in less high-minded ways they are still revered.

One Summer I came up here and heard, before I got to them, the echoing of many voices, squeals and screams, sounding as if the rocks themselves were shouting out. It was a party of school children learning how to climb and others below, weaselling through crevices.

A young boy was out with his Dad and I overheard their discussion of where they might sit for the best view, where they might be comfortable and where there might be a shelf for their flask. A group of women and children walked past and spread out blankets at the foot of the rocks for a picnic. That day the stones were alive with enjoyment.

The Wainstones can be approached many ways but the proper way is from Bilsdale to the south, gradually arriving in Garfitt Gap and closing in on their distinctive profile. This is also the way people of the early Neolithic purposefully approached them. How do we know? Well, a remarkable discovery has been made by local field archaeologist Brian Smith and his associates. Brian has found and described a semi-circular pathway marked, along its one kilometre length, by cup and ring marked and specially arranged pointer stones, which end just beneath and looking up to the Wainstones.

I have traced this myself and Brian has shown me even more recently discovered marks. It is really exciting, like decoding a secret meaning, seeing how one marked stone leads to another to form a ritualised pathway set up over 5000 years ago. It is a small scale Simonside in Northumberland or Rombold's Moor Ilkley, both bigger examples of early hunter-farmer's sacred landscapes.

Here the stone ridge provides a natural set of megalithic totems, as good as any Stonehenge, with no backache required. Interestingly, there are no prehistoric marks at all on the Wainstones themselves, perhaps a further confirmation of their sacred importance.

Most dramatic of all the surviving motifs here, are those on three of the boulders that lie on their own in the field directly below the

Wainstones. These have large basin hollows, probably natural in origin, but enhanced and scooped out further and noticeably joined and added to with cup marks and rings and pecked channels, so that they become, in wet weather, water catcher and flow directors, perhaps once symbolising the flow of life itself.

Whatever their meaning, they invite ritual and I cannot resist, whenever I visit, tossing in a pebble or coin, pouring in water to make them come to life or, floating a snowball in their meltwaters. They seem to bring together the elemental nature of the stones and the hills around, in their lost iconography.

Snow time is particularly revealing up here. It's not just people who weasel and climb on the rocks. I remember visiting here in fine, undisturbed Christmas snow, seeing the perfect imprint of a bird's wing on the very top of one of the pillars like a white, crystallised fan: following the print marks of ermined stoats: coming across the severed hind leg of a hare on top of one of the basin stones. There is always something about the Wainstones that is inexplicable.

Strange as it may seem, this day, I am almost disappointed by the fog lifting, for I crave the intimacy it brings, the mystery of its gossamer cover, which seems to assimilate the flow of the rock formations into one body.

It descends again, wetter now, a mizzling emulsion, prickling exposed skin. I meander up and down Cold Moor, the next hill across and look back on the Wainstones and Garfitt Pass below. I take in their overall shape and layout, the arc of rock art beneath and their boulders with water features, like mini landscapes, glinting in the low light.

By contrast, the day I revisit them after my hip operation, it is a brazen, sunny day.

I carefully climb the steep path to the ridge, it being only three weeks since 'the cut'. The views and energy of the place give me strength. I reacquaint myself with familiar spots and satisfied, start back and as I do one slight movement to my left makes me stop and stare.

A tiny lizard, match box sized, comes back out to sun itself on a rock, under a forest of heather. I have to watch it with my reading glasses on, it is so small and so close.

It is a tincture of lizard, pin head, beady eye, sinuous tail, five spread fingers on each foot, its body tingling in the sunlight, jewelled in gold and jade, a thin, dark, meridian line along its side. I have seen many lizards in my time, sea-swimming dragons, some that change colour and others with blue heads and orange legs, but this little fellow is the best I've ever seen: essence of lizard concentrated in miniature.

What is it, I ponder, about the minute and fine details we encounter in big landscapes that makes them so important? Small creatures such as this, living their lives in microcosm, within the bigger landscapes we walk in, hold our attention, as their presence is a pin prick of intensity: a tiny shrew moving under snow: the peacock eyes on a butterfly wing: the cardinal beetle, framed by a single cobble: a mini waterscape of riverine, lake and tarn, recognised in the top of a single field boulder.

Through these small lives we perceive, in abbreviated detail, the full immensity and multi layered nature of existence, all ultimately, universally connected. Big thoughts come from little things.

So as the mist envelops me once more, I walk back up through and past the stones. I follow the snaking, slippery path, breathing in the vapours of rock and fine air as I go, uplifted, as ever I am, by my encounter and memories of the Wainstones.

*(Redcar and Marske Beach, with Fred, 1968 to 1998)*

# Our Beach

I found a dead body once, on our beach, lapping in the waves. Or I should say we found it, my Uncle Fred and me, on an early morning walk before school. It was a grim and exciting discovery, but not that surprising. Fred, my brother Chris, and I found everything that washed up here: a catalogue of finds and pickings from a sea, washing the natural and the unnatural in and out with the tide.

Our beach is not exotic or palm fringed. It is in Marske by the Sea, Northumbria, characterised by cold, slashing winds all year round. You bend into it. It is a flatland, once loved by speed record breakers and sand kiters. It is longitudinally zoned, from fishing boats snagged in deep, soft sand at the top, to sheens of pebbles and shale, straggling deposits of seaweed and jetsam, thin sinuous ridges, pools and wave-washed, fine sands, streaked with sea coal and sloping gently into the hard, cold North Sea. Reddish, boulder clay cliffs and dunes sewn together with marram grass are its backdrop.

Whatever the conditions, we were there. Uncle Fred patrolled it several times a day as self-appointed beach caretaker, eyes down, poking the strandline with his stick, seeing what had washed up that day.

Dead things were of daily interest. Oiled seabirds were checked for rings, which if cut off and sent to the London Natural History Museum, revealed their secret lives: an oystercatcher ringed in Norway 32 years ago, a 14 year old puffin from Iceland. Skulls, feet, wings and feathers were taken as booty, to feed a natural history obsession. We marvelled at great dead gannets, broken by the sea storms and the little auks, desiccated by the salt wind.

When a cetacean or seal washed up we held our own inquiry on the spot. Any markings to indicate cause of death? Maybe the dolphin had been hit by a boat's propeller, the seal killed by a blow to the head with a gaff? Perhaps the pilot whale was just old and disorientated, off course and drowned in the shallow? Could anyone ever mistake it for a mermaid, we mused? More importantly, could we wrestle a tooth from its jaw and try to carve it, like the old seadogs did?

We didn't fancy whale meat. But some things were definitely edible. Fred would spot splashing in the wave edge and we'd walk fast toward it. Sea bream, washed into shallow water, these perpendicular flatties really were out of their depth and a stick soon turned them into bounty. Thick, bony steaks, eaten later with big fat chips and too much salt and pepper were delicious.

We got out the shrimp net now and then, bringing up the see-through, black eyed, whiskery crustaceans from their sandy beds, scooping them into buckets and boiling them pink, before chewing on their 'fizzoggs'.

Even greater prizes were to be had at 'The Flashes', the rocks at Redcar that marked the beach end, laying themselves out to dry every low tide. Crabs could be hooked and even lobsters, from deeper recesses off the end. We recalled time and again the mythical 'Lince's lobster', monster from the deep, caught by the local fishing family, just offshore here. It filled the fishmonger's window from one end to the other; photographs were taken. It really was six foot long, in my child's mind anyway.

Another time, box after box of sea biscuits littered the sands, all in waterproof foiled tins, ship's emergency rations stuffed with vitamins and as dry as chalk. They lasted years and fed visitors and dogs alike.

There was money and romance to be found in our beachcomber wanderings. Most lucrative of all was finding the plastic, red disc trailers, weighted sea current trackers thrown into the sea by fisheries' researchers to mark out the effect of currents along the shore. Their return fetched a £1 reward and Fred and I found a lot, more even than the fishermen, chasing into the sea in their tractors.

The 'romance' came in the form of messages in bottles, in all languages, Spanish, Greek, even hieroglyphics that teachers couldn't decipher. I'd write in hope to hardly understood people caught up in the tide of life in far flung places, with no replies ever received as yet.

Big rubber floats served as bouncy 'kangaroo balls', wicker ship fenders, as big as a boy, as garden ornaments, wood for every use you can think of. I still eat my tea off a yacht cabin door panel of mahogany. We even found a home-made harp, strung with cat gut.

There were holed witches' stones and fossil 'devil's toenails' to collect, sponges and sea potatoes to bottle till rancid, urchins and angry, spiked weaver fish to avoid.

Other people walked here, but no one else found and feasted on these serendipitous sea finds like us. If they did, we never saw them.

Oh, and that human body we found. To anyone who revels in the forensic you would be disappointed at our lack of interest. We did not disturb the scene, but walked slowly on past it. But not before seeing it was so blown up, it looked like it had a white, rubber, diving suit on.

As far as we could tell, it smelled of the sea, not like the half rotten dolphins we'd seen. There were red wheals where the fishes had sucked and no finger nails, or did I make that up? Did I really tell the kids at school, that I thought I'd seen webbed fingers, a tail?

We found out from the Evening Gazette it had been a woman washed overboard from a Russian trawler. There were shades of the KGB.

It may have been one of the most memorable things we found, but it wasn't the most exciting thing we ever found on our beach, by a long way.

*(Loftus and towns across the North East)*

# Seymour (and other Hawks)

Sparrow hawks are pretty common nowadays and they are the birds of prey I clock most often and which add a dash of excitement as I too fly through the North East, criss-crossing town and country, going about my business.

They inhabit the green verges between towns, intrepid bird missiles launching between buildings, gliding through gardens, spiralling overhead. Occasionally you surprise one with its kill pinned to the ground in its talons. It will not be easily scared away, intent on its meal.

At close quarters you are stunned by its brutality and its beauty, the male especially with its dark blue back and wings, orange tinted breast and wild eyes.

Hawks were fine-tuned by evolution, over millennia, to be sharp eyed, sprint flying killers, homing in on their unsuspecting prey, small birds, as if from nowhere. Only sometimes, even they, in our topsy-turvy world, get into trouble and need a helping hand.

Hence the tale of 'Seymour', who one day flew in through the door of the opticians in Loftus High Street and concussed himself on the back wall. He was placed in a box to recover.

The Herald and Post reported the incident with the irony it deserved and described the mayhem as the bird, christened Seymour (as in see-more) "launched himself out of the box and flew in circles around the shop. Optometrist, John Prouse, heard the commotion and had to duck to avoid the bird as he came out of his examination room."Seymour made a full recovery and was returned to the skies and as the newspaper concluded, "at least he knows where the opticians is now if he needs any further help".

Birds of prey do get into trouble, often on a collision course with our unnatural world. Once I zoomed past a sparrow hawk sitting like a statue on the side of a busy road, just missing the traffic. I was able to turn around and stop and it let me pick it up, it was so stunned. The bird had either been swept up by a passing vehicle or stilled by a strong gust of wind, on this very blustery day.

She was a beautiful, female hawk. I held her on my knee and examined her, carefully extending her wings and feeling for any obvious injury. She allowed me to touch her long black and white barred tail. Her golden and black eyes searched for meaning. Sharp talons started to push into my thigh. She was in fine shape and uninjured and, after a short rest, flew out of my hands re-joining the air she belonged in, leaving me with a feeling of total privilege.

Another time I rescued a kestrel from a gutter, its wing this time obviously damaged and looking like some chestnut coloured giant bat, screeching hopelessly. Ensconced in my coat I swept it up and away. It was treated at a local falconry centre and was eventually released. I have driven past that exact spot many times since and often I see a pair of kestrels, hunched in the trees or hovering over the fields, a welcome sight, as they are not as common as they were. Northumberland remains a stronghold.

Raptors often reflect subtle changes in the environment humans have affected, such as the pesticide DDT which saw the dramatic demise of peregrines in the 1960s and the poisoning and other persecutions that affect red kites and many others. No one yet knows why kestrels are in decline but you can be sure it will be something we have changed for the worse.

However, near the start of this journey I watched the antics of a pair in the Cheviots, calling from crags, wing batting the unwanted attentions of crows. They are making a comeback on our road verges across Northumbria, perhaps as a result of less assiduous grass cutting from cash cut Councils. Often Northumbria bucks the national trends in species decline, as we still have more wild places than most.

Come to think of it, maybe its luck, maybe I'm on the lookout, but I have also found and tried to help fallen buzzards in Devon, a red kite on the North York Moors and part of my first job was to protect breeding peregrines. There have been several more sparrow hawks too that I have found stunned or killed, often having banged into windows they thought were clear fly-throughs. I have also picked up young owls and placed them back in their roadside trees from where they had wandered.

Sometimes I feel like their human guardian. I've a definite affinity with our fast flying owls and hawks. The flow patterns of these predators coincide with the cyclical car journeys I regularly make. Thankfully, I've managed to avoid doing them any damage myself.

Yes, they are quick and observant, but they are not always careful. In their haste they become, like we often do, unstuck and need a nurturing hand.

*(Mulgrave Woods,*
*Wengen and Sandsend)*

## Alpine-Mulgrave

Like a missile the black woodpecker undulated toward my mother-in-law, threatening to take her head off at the shoulders and she was totally unaware of it!

We slowly threaded our way up the forested slopes of Biglenalp above Wengen, in the Bernese Oberland. It was steep and challenging so I had looked back to see if Mary was keeping up and I caught this scene, stilled in my memory ever since.

Thankfully it missed her and thudded instead onto the side of a massive fir tree. It stood magnificent, bracketed onto the bark with its enormous zygodactylic feet, a woodpecker of such scale and majesty it seemed hardly related to the garden-visiting greater spotteds we fed at home. In fact it looked Jurassic.

This was just one of many ornithological surprises we experienced on a late Summer walking break in the Swiss Alps and I am reminded of it every time we visit a favourite walk of ours back home, but more of that later. My head is still in the Alps, big mountains, big wildlife, and an alpine assortment designed for life in the extreme environment that is 'mountain'.

It is nutcrackers next that grab our attention. Bird of children's fable and ballet legend they are top class corvids, all suited out in their brown and white speckled plumage, with startled expressions. We find them chasing down the chestnuts, living up to their names, snapping walnuts in half, flying from tree to tree in the alpine orchards of Wengenalp.

Way above this scene, in the very highest parts of the mountain, where snow lingers long, the snow finches are at home and walking becomes climbing, we discover a whole new world of natural history. As our endurance fades, we are buoyed by the sight of marmots living in their glacier-sided 'setts', sunning themselves in the burning light. Constant companions are the alpine choughs, their yellow beaks and red legs adding a cartoon like appearance to their musical, chiming voices.

And higher still, a pin prick in the sky, a mere shadow cast in an alpine meadow, the bone-cracking, marrow-sucking Lammergeyer vulture, drops its bones of freshly dead chamois onto rocks around us, to rattle, split and then to alight on. Black-masked and long-tongued to lick out the marrowfat, this rare sighting was a mountain blessing.

Another day we are even lucky enough to spy the famously elusive wall creeper on a high rock slope, a red and silver explosion in the afternoon sun.

All this came back to me as I walked, not in the Alps, but in the beautiful woods of Mulgrave, on the North Yorkshire coast. The setting evokes such memories as it is, in part, an alpine scene in miniature, with its stands of spruce and fir, interspersed with rowan, maple and oak.

It even has its own mountain hut in a grassy clearing, a 'mountain' stream torrents down from the moors nearby. The hut is a shed for a grass cutter but I long to sleep in there and dream of The Alps again, the great climb up the Obersteinburg, the wonderful, unreal beauty of the Tchingelhorn Hotel on the way up at Trachsellauenen, seeing melanistic red squirrels and Ibex on the same path.

But I am mountain dreaming again. There are none of these or black woodpeckers here of course. These woods are tame by comparison, but there are other things: goshawk to be glimpsed: stoats, foxes and

145

badgers: sea trout in the beck: even otters hereabouts and roe deer in both places.

It's not quite the alpine set, but it is stimulating in its own way and more easily accessed.

Like many visitors, I often start out from, or end up at 'Wits End'. Few who take repast here are actually in mental crisis, rather it is an evocative tag for a charming café. At the foot of Lythe Bank, with its back to the sea and cliffs, it is more a bolt hole for hikers and strollers, than a psychiatrist's surgery. Perhaps it is a bit of both. Good food, sea air, gentle exercise and a nice view are all good for our wellbeing. The café is also the site of the old butcher's and where the otter hounds used to be kennelled.

To think otters were still being hunted in Teesdale in the 1970s! Luckily, after years of persecution and pollution led to their near extinction, they are back on most Northumbrian rivers and they returned here before most other parts of England, coming down through Scotland across The Borders and into Northumberland, spreading south, a pattern so common for many species, across this land.

It's not long before you are tempted to explore further, down to the foreshore to fathom Sandsend's rock pools, to look for jet, fondle a fossil.

But if the tide's in, you're going nowhere. A rough sea at Sandsend is like a multiple geyser, vented explosively over the sea wall, dramatic, oceanic. Then it's out with the camera or just your eyes, to stare and take in the power of the tidal flow's performance.

Many come here just to walk by the sea and comb its sands, traversing the land sea edge. It is an easy way into the Jurassic cliff line of North Yorkshire, the so called 'Dinosaur Coast': a place to sit and dream about the plesiosaurs and ichthyosaurs, ammonites and belemnites, all the extinct, marine creatures that lived in the warmer seas 200 million years ago in these parts, their remains sandwiched in the rocks around you.

I prefer to explore the two valley hamlets of orange-roofed cottages, which channel into delightful and some say enchanted, woods. The Mulgrave valleys interconnect and confuse like a labyrinthine forest. Legend and mythology lie deep amongst their sylvan beauty and meandering becks.

The link between land and the sea is aptly demonstrated by these watery, wooded ways. They flow toward the sea, of course, but the sea trout and salmon go against the watery grain; it is a two way flow. Seldom-seen otters inhabit both environs, leaving their Parma-violet smelling spraint on rocks and bridges, treading where we cannot trace.

The woods are not a little exotic in themselves, a lovely blend of the natural broadleaf woodland along the becks (with a nice spindle grove, alder carr and oakwoods) augmented by unusual (try paper birch) parkland specimen planting, veteran beech, ash trees, majestic Douglas fir and other conifers, creating its alpine character.

All this is added to by its history, its 18th Century estate bridges and carriageways, Mulgrave Hall itself in its landscaped grounds. It even has its own romanticised castle ruin, a partly restored 13th Century castle (and an even earlier motte and bailey one, hidden further up) situated on a tall river cliff, visible from gaps in the trees, from afar. It is the perfect place for a picnic, or meditation on the diversity of these woods.

You might not see black woodpeckers or wall creeper but you have a great chance of seeing and hearing their relatives, the great spotted and the big, canary-coloured, green woodpecker, the nuthatch and tree creeper.

The estate is now, as it has been since Norman times, a privileged seat of Lords, kept for exclusive sport and gaming. The likes of famous models, and even Madonna, are helicoptered in for a weekend pheasant shoot. There are industrial numbers of pheasants in the thicker woods which, like their pursuers, startle and annoy. But still the woods retain their ancient and rich character.

Delving deeper into the history of these woods, you might be surprised to find references to an Indian Prince and an elephant that, in the early 19th Century, could be seen walking these paths and woods. The scene was brilliantly re-created a few years ago in a memorable outdoor drama I am proud to say I had a supportive part in. Northumbria, as ever, is full of surprises!

Discovering the alpine set is one thing. Re-discovering it, intertwined with the similarities and differences I find in my local environment, is an even bigger revelation.

That we can inhabit these places any time we need to revitalise our spirits and re-charge our imaginations, is amazing.

*(Marske and Saltburn Banks)*

# Agar's Gap

Who the hell Agar was I don't know. Maybe it will come to light but he had a gap named after him. A gap that is a hollow, or 'howle', a narrow gulley leading down to the beach, between boulder clay, grass mop-topped cliffs and dunes, what we locally call 'the Banks'. These lie between Marske and Saltburn on the North East coast. Like 'Blue Mountain' at the other end, it is a local landmark, everybody knows Agar's Gap, if not Agar.

It's a gap down past the toe-end of the biggest of the clay cliffs and an old route from farm to sea, a fisherman's track or even a smuggler's pass, its true origins lost in time.

There is a sense of importance about it. Its big, rounded, pock-marked face looks across at you as you look at it. I remember when foxes lived here, breeding and parading themselves and their half-eaten prey, which they had scavenged between sea and land. Before that there was obviously a badger sett here, its structure still vaguely visible in the grass-covered soil heaps and little flattened platforms, next to long collapsed entrances to their underground labyrinth. Now only rabbits reside here and hungry weasels pass through.

More than anything it is a gap of reflection, a stopping point for local people and their dogs, of quiet discourse between person and place, just far enough away from habitation for us to feel unburdened. Its hollows are accommodating, loafing holes, for sky and sea watching, haloed in a haze of rough grass and meadow flower pollen. It is an edge line between beach and cultivation.

The stonechat is guardian of the gap, perching and patrolling this scrubby territory of blackthorn and bramble, trimmed by the sharp, salt wind and clinging, like dry green scabs, to battered clay slopes. A small rivulet winds down to the sand, becoming entangled and strewn with beaching, where the land tip toes into the high tide.

I have seen other things here too: lost woodpeckers, desperately seeking woodland in winter. Kestrels hover incessantly over its knotted grass and gorse. You can hear the high-pitched whistles of shrews hidden in the sward and the skylarks that nest here, twirling in the sky and dropping to slink the back way into their knotted grass nests.

Sea shrouds the place, lends its complexion to the land. Mist creeps in to mask the gap's presence, misting it in a fret, blasting it with storms, venting its spume upon it, dissipating its damp, salt breath.

And the sun warms it too. Its south easterly slopes are a retreat, soaking up the warmth. This is where the dogs pant and sunbathe, tongues lolling, and where walkers sit back and stretch out, take off hats and gloves, take out handkerchiefs to wipe their wind-torn eyes and noses, a place of calm repose with the ferocious sea just around the corner.

Agar's Gap is a point half way between two seaside towns - a small pass, or hollow, where warm reflection and enlightened contemplation come together somehow, creating some light within. So thank God for Agar, whoever he was, and more especially, for his gap.

*(Kettleness and Hayburn Wyke,
North Yorkshire heritage coast)*

## Down Kettleness

There's an intangible quality here as I drop down the cliffs, terrace by slope-slip-terrace, into their depths, delving beneath the Earth's fissile skin.

The light is hanging there waiting. The stark brightness makes the iris open wide and sometimes there is a darker, heavier atmosphere, saturated with the sulphurous stink of bituminous rocks, slowly and continuously releasing into the air.

The salt of the sea comes up to meet me, as I touch down on the curve of shore backed by these steep cliffs. The cliffs sparkle with pyrite and leak alum sulphate, its milkiness forming an oily film on shining rock pools. The shale shatters and peels to reveal impressions of the rocky remains of an ammonite sea.

I muse along the tideline and pick up a fist sized 'cannonball' nodule which I crack with a hammer blow to find a perfectly preserved ammonoid inside. It is like a fossil nautilus shell, with its sickle shaped whorls etched in fool's gold. Cradled in my hand it is a touchstone of Earth history.

Then, there's the jet, which I find bits of wedged under boulders, glistening in thin black seams in the rock face, or as sea-polished nuggets, shiny as plastic. The focus of the jewellery trade for thousands of years, they were a Bronze Age fad, as well as Victorian mourning wear. I remember seeing similar bits of unworked material from an excavation of a Roman workshop in fields behind Loftus, collected like this and ready to be worked. Jet has timeless qualities. It is a symbol of life's distilling powers: grainless and metamorphosed,

Jurassic, monkey puzzle driftwood, concentrated dinosaur time-tar.

Everyone who makes this drop down the wet and slimy cliff face is looking for something: fossils, jet, beach combings or fish and bait from the sea. Some will find much more, peace and stillness, a raging range of elements or a retreat from the worst weather in the back of an old alum hole and a sense of being in a place apart, a bay of days with no easy way out. It is a place to be calmed for a while, to tune into the sea and the ageless cliffs.

I walk around the corner, past the stone pillar, a small stack made by man and sea and follow the iron seams that run kidney red across the foreshore, like giant veins: past the 'swans foot mollusc beds': past the 'pecten seam', to the 'doggers' and onto the massive rockfall of deltaic sandstones, where I can see ancient plant remains and re-visit the footprint of a dinosaur I know of, in a fallen boulder.

The rock face is sheer above me now and raining bits down, I need to be careful as I venture on. There are wrecks aplenty about to remind me of the ferocity of this coast. I sit on an old anchor, amid the metal shards of one such ship. I too feel shipwrecked, stilled by this raw beauty, my head all out at sea.

A little later, I find myself standing, holding a small, rock disc in my palm. It is hard to register that it is a single vertebra from an ichthyosaur. The chances of finding it at all, amongst all the pebbles and rocks of this place are tiny, a rock bone from an extinct, reptilian dolphin.

Fossils allow us to time travel back millions of years. Yet it is impossible to think of Earth's time continuum in human terms, our lives being so short. Where and what will we be I wonder in another 200,000 years, never mind millions? Will civilisation have turned into fossilisation, or will we have entirely succumbed, as a species, to automation?

On the way back up I follow the hollowed, saddle-shaped trod, laid by alum workers and jet miners and feel their presence now as I struggle upwards, my feet sliding back with the weight of my rock-filled rucksack.

But however fortunate I have been, 'the Ness' always keeps something back. Much lies undiscovered underneath, sandwiched deep in its strata. Eventually, they will be exhumed from their rock beds, all will be revealed. Whole skeletons from these cliffs grace the cabinets of museum collections all over the world.

There is only one Kettleness, one of the most evocative places on the whole Northumbrian coastline. Close rivals though are the 'Wykes' of this Jurassic coast, between Staithes and Scarborough.

What is a Wyke? It is a dialect term for a small bay, about eight of which can be found, from Brackenbury and Loop Wykes in the north, to Deepgrove and Maw and Blea Wykes in the south.

The most stunning of all is Hayburn Wyke, near Ravenscar. Picture perfect, a half hemisphere of a bay guarded by two perfectly balanced rocky promontories, with a backdrop of ancient woodland and its own dramatic waterfall onto a boulder beach. It even has its own set of three-toed dino-prints, if you can find them. An incredible combination in one small place, a 'wonder Wyke'.

Walking down through the woods towards the Wyke is like being on the set of the 'French Lieutenant's Woman' film, so alike are the cliff-line woods of Dorset and North Yorkshire here. There is a romance about the place. Last time I visited, I cut a special, twisting staff from the woods and sat gazing out from beneath a beautiful, almost Buddha-shaped tree. It is a place of myth and mystery inviting natural ceremony.

One more thing, if Kettleness has the best restaurant just up the road at Goldsborough (The Fox and Hounds), then Hayburn Wyke has the best pub. There is something of the 'old merry England' to entering a pub, almost within and of the woods, at the start of the path that leads to this amazing Wyke-world. It is the place to reflect on the beauty that lies beyond.

The Ness and the Wyke are like manifestations of our environmental fantasies, being so perfect. It is their liminal qualities I have encountered in Northumbria time and again, their aesthetic harmony. You are acutely aware of the depth of time and yet you are constantly drawn back to the beauty in the moment. Ironically, when stood amongst these rocks of great age, time actually matters not a jot down the Ness or in the Wyke.

*(Maritime Alps and Lythe Church)*

## Bears and Wolves

I know how it feels when the hunter becomes the hunted, to sense the eyes of a predator watching you unseen. Once, on the side of a mountain stream, I came across a very fresh kill of a roe deer, still bleeding, at my feet.

I had disturbed some big carnivore's meal and I could feel that it was still close by. The hair on my neck stood up, my heart pounded and I was unsure whether to stay very still or run, overcome by a mixture of thrill and fear.

I turned slowly around and expected, half hoped, to see a lynx. Wolves and bears were, I thought, very unlikely, for though I stood in the Valle de Loup, the Wolf Valley, they had been hunted out years ago. The Maritime Alps felt too safe, a throw from the Riviera. I did not know then of their re-colonisation from Italy.

At first I saw nothing. Then, there was a movement, an indistinct grey and rufous flash of dog-like haunch and tail. A shadow of the wolf ran off into the trees and a shiver ran through me.

This must have been a regular occurrence for the people of the Northumbrian landscape from prehistory right up to the 16th Century, when the last wolves thrived in our woods, as late as 1700. Place names such as Wooler, Howl Moor and Wolf Pit Slack tell of this. In Baysdale, in the North York Moors, rents were paid in wolf heads and skins in mediaeval times. They remained long after the brown bear, which was hunted out by the Iron Age, though remained commonplace on the nearby continent, for centuries after.

We get a taste of our prehistoric ecology, from the footsteps preserved in that peat at Hauxley, on the Northumberland coast, where the prints of aurochs and wild boar are preserved alongside human footprints.

In the times of Celtic Saints, Anglo Saxon settlement and Viking raids, Nature was feared and revered in equal measure. Perhaps these were the last of the primeval, greenwood days when a real sense of the wild prevailed. However wild our landscape is today, it is tame by comparison with what it was like hundreds or thousands of years ago.

All this occurs to me now, as I stand in the cliff top, church yard of Lythe, near Whitby, taking in the scene of woods running down to the sea. For, farfetched as it may seem, in the church here, there is an enduring vestige of Northumbrian wildwood times and their foreboding inhabitants. In this little corner of Northumbria, there are still a few wolves and bears about.

These actually take the form of stone-carved figures on the remains of what was an exclusive 10th Century Viking-Saxon graveyard. They are impressive nonetheless, if not directly threatening. On one, the stretched open jaws of a bear form bookends to a 'hogback' gravestone; another depicts a simple, human figure being torn apart by two stylised wolves. There are also birds and a serpent. These few 'zoomorphs' give a hint of Nature and people in turbulent times.

There is a lot of history concentrated in this one small place. It captures a time when the Celtic Kingdom was falling into decline, following Viking raids and colonisation down the coast. These stone carvings are a mix of Anglo-Saxon Christian influences, blended with that of the Pagan incomer. Scandinavian craft-workers had traded on nearby Sandsend beach and ended up living, sculpting and dying here.

The symbolism is even more enlightening, hinting at a Nature-based mythology. The bear is the Norse guardian of the dead, revered for its strength and its sensitivity. On the one hand its furs were worn to imbue the warrior with great bravery and ferocity and on the other, the mother bear was noted for her patience and transformative powers, literally, 'licking into shape' her new born, formless cubs.

The wolf is seen as the feared 'Fenrir', a giant wolf monster, killer of the weak. It is ironic that in reality wolves rarely attack or kill people. Neither I nor the Vikings or Saxons had anything really to fear from the wolf.

Standing in the graveyard outside, I begin to notice, in the bushes and trees, many small birds, a handful of tiny goldcrests, at least half a dozen robins and a lot of blackbirds. They have surely just migrated in from just across the North Sea on this windy 'fall' day. The churchyard is a natural refuge.

How appropriate and what a lovely bit of synergy, that these vagrant Scandinavian birds should hole up here, where a thousand years ago, human migrants were adding colour and expressing in stone their particular feelings about their wild lore. This is one small corner of Northumbria where the natural, the cultural and the mythological are still entwined.

*(Whitby, North Berwick, Peebles, Morpeth and Leeds)*

# Whales' Bones

Old whale bones just keep turning up. The famous, whale jawbone arch that welcomes visitors to Whitby's West Cliff and are a nod to its whaling past is taken as read: likewise, the local landmark of North Berwick's conical hill, Berwick Law, on the coast along from Edinburgh, with its successive sets of jaws, mounted there since 1709, now alas, replaced by a fibreglass replica.

But there are others too, secreted into places across the North East, in what seem unlikely locations, which make you question why they are there at all.

Driving through the Borders, near Peebles, I came across the whale bone entrance to Netherud House, a stately home, the bones placed there over a century ago and remounted in the 1960s.

Diverted, during flood defence works, through the back streets of Morpeth, I was equally surprised to come across a fine, whale jawbone specimen guarding the entrance to two suburban properties. They looked like they had been there a while and I noticed a place called 'Jawbone yard' nearby. I thought of the postman passing under these every day as part of his, or her deliveries.

To locals in Rothwell, near Leeds, in West Yorkshire, whale bone jaws have always marked the Wood Lane crossroads, or thereabouts, since the early 19th Century and still do.

Maybe the oldest, surviving whale bones that were ever on display outdoors in this region (there are lots in museums) are those recently rediscovered by archaeologist Barry Mead, in Cresswell, on Druridge Bay.

Whilst excavating the remains of the now demolished Cresswell Hall, he came across a set of whale bones, including vertebrae, teeth and ribs. He traced them back to the display of a whole sperm whale skeleton, which had beached off Cresswell and been rendered and displayed, on a specially made plinth in the Hall's conservatory, in the 1820s, remaining there until the 1930s.

A number of species are represented here, but are hard to identify. The first Whitby bones of the 1960s were of a fin whale, killed by Norwegian whalers in the Antarctic, the newer ones, erected in 2002, were a little more eco-friendly, the jaws of a bowhead whale, killed legally by Alaskan Inuit, in 1996.

These are indicators of what was an immense whaling industry down the North East coast, since the 17th Century. The seaside gems of Whitby, Berwick and other places up and down the coast, were once stinking, smouldering, flensing sites for thousands of slaughtered whales, their baleen and blubber then being turned into an array of grisly, but needed products. It was an unsustainable harvest across the world, over centuries, which led to their widespread protection and relative rarity today, especially inshore.

It makes me want to know more, not about the industry but what may have become of the whales and other cetaceans off our coast today. Whilst we have no really big animals left in Northumbria, unless you count the Chillingham cattle, wild goats and deer, the only real megafauna we have are still out there at sea and are not only seals.

Yes there are whales and their relatives, several species, regularly visiting these shores and making a comeback. Sometimes they wash up. I still remember the pong and the pink, resinous fleshiness of a massive, rotting sperm whale I went to see down Hawsker Bottoms in the 1990s. What an amazing animal, the length of a bus with its great tail flukes, from which a local artist was taking a paint print: a tiny mouth and eye, compared to its bulk: its delicate jutting jaw, with beautiful, conical teeth, designed for chewing its prey of deep sea squid. Others died in the shallows and washed up at Redcar in 2011 and at Druridge in 2013.

As boys, we used to sometimes find smaller whales on the beach, pilot whale, minke and a beaked whale, I recall.

Having taken trips deliberately to see whales off Iceland, western Scotland and other places abroad and being delighted by their presence and relative abundance, I never seriously looked for them here until recent years. I probably missed a lot!

It is not like the Icelandic seas off Reykavik, with whales in every direction I looked, as well as porpoise and dolphin. But there are now regular and impressive sightings off the coast from Berwick to The Farnes, Tynemouth to the Tees and from Whitby to Flamborough. There are now even whale-watching trips from Whitby, where, in autumn in particular, the migration of minke and fin whales seems to follow in the wake of shoals of mackerel and herring, all signs that our living seas, though still vulnerable, are making a recovery.

Humpback whales and minke whales have also been seen off The Farnes and there are rumours of orca, look out seals! Tynemouth has its pod of bottle-nosed dolphins, just offshore and porpoises are seen in many places.

I have come across Northumbria's whales now on several recent occasions, not just dead ones, as in a recent, cliff-top wander near Port Mulgrave.

I spot a fishing boat a little way out of the harbour and watch as a large, dark, shining body rises near and appears to follow it. The boat turns in little circles to track the curve. It is big, nearly half the length of the boat, low and dark, but has no obvious fin. It is surely too big for a dolphin.

After seeing it several more times I am nearly convinced. I set off for a cup of tea at The Ship in Port Mulgrave village. Just as I enter the café and reply to the proprietor's friendly question of, 'Have you seen much then?' with, 'I think I have seen a whale', a twitter feed message comes in on the café computer, reporting that a young minke whale has been reported and followed, just off the harbour at Port Mulgrave next to a fishing boat. You can't get better synergy or quicker corroboration than that.

The summer of 2013 was a good time for spotting cetaceans. I couldn't believe my eyes one afternoon in Sandsend when, just beyond the breakers, in the middle of the reasonably busy beach, a large dolphin swam in and out of the shallows for half an hour. It must have come close to beaching itself, it got so close to shore, before beating its way back out again, obviously following shoals of fish. I was surprised that no one else around seemed to notice this big, shining, grey-white animal, showing its fin and flukes, corkscrewing around. There were more out to sea all that week, but none came as close as this one.

Was it being playful or foolish? Talking of which, off the top of Boulby cliff, there is a fixed rope to the shore used by fishermen and others to precariously lower themselves down the cliff to the shore below and to carry beach combed objects back up. It's the 'old fisherman's rope trick', there being several in small, inaccessible bays along the coast, which, in one or two places, give you a unique view of the coast if you are daft enough to risk it. Please don't try after reading this if you find one. There is a more official and professionally secured one off the end of the Sandsend railway which is the safest, if you must, but still watch your footing and the tide. I speak from embarrassing experience.

From the Boulby one you get a bird's eye view of a large platform of flat, grassy cliff before the final drop to the foreshore. When the tide comes in and is calm, it feels like sitting on the edge of an endless briny lake. One birthday I sat here alone and watched a whole school of porpoises, perhaps thirty in all, surfacing and diving just offshore, fishing for inshore mackerel or sprats. It was one hell of a present. The only hitch was that I left my binoculars at the bottom and had to climb the precarious rope up and down twice. It was worth it afterwards.

You may find your own hotspots. The Farnes, Tynemouth and Flamborough headlands and Filey Brigg are renowned, spotting places onshore. If you have the stomach for it and want to get up close, take a boat. I am no sailor these days, but I may be there too. Having experienced the smell of fishy flume from a close-up whale and having my hair stand on end as they sidled alongside a boat I was in, exchanging glances, I can vouch, that getting up close to whales could get addictive. It is truly magical and the excitement can even overcome sea sickness.

Last November, I sat next to a chap in the pub who had just got off the Whitby whale-watching boat trip and the photographs he had of minke whales were impressive.

These beasts of Northumbrian waters are out there. Interesting curiosities they may be, but you don't have to settle any more for museum displays of skeletons and harpoons, denoting our dubious relationship with whales in the past. After the amount of whaling that went on and the effect that must have had on the marine ecosystem, we can witness for ourselves their recent, increasing return to our inshore waters and reflect on the fact that we are now hunting them harmlessly, with cameras and binoculars.

Photos and memories of these beautiful and sensitive sea giants will be the legacy now, not just their bones, symbols of a brutal past.

*To the wet* **Feet** *of it all, down in the rolling chalk and marshes of south Northumbria*

# Humber-Woldland

The far, southern reaches of the joined-up landscape of my Northumbria is so different to the northern lands that, at first, I hesitated to include them. However, as I have explored them further, I am reminded and introduced to reasons for their being very much part of the network of connected Nature and culture of the North East, not least because, as a child, this is where I first learnt about northern Nature and it is where the land runs itself out into the North Sea. They are firmly on my mind map.

These are the flatlands, marshes, fens and lowland peatscapes of the Humberhead levels, wetland edges to the Trent, the Derwent and the Humber, around Goole and the geomorphological wonder that is Spurn Point. Here is the last, proper upland of the north, again so very different, flowing chalk lands, the northern Downs, 'The Wolds'.

The Wolds were the playground of my youth, a place of holidays, Aunts and Uncles, a countryside seen through rose-tinted spectacles, a place of rural idyll, played out among the charming villages of Sledmere, Wetwang, Fimber, Driffield and Duggleby, before it became 'Hockney-esque'.

This region is the Ying to the Yang of the Northumbrian uplands and it is wild in other, more subtle ways. It is historically connected too to the north, as it was the place the Celtic priests travelled through, to set up monasteries as far south as the Essex marshes, impressed as they were by the area's seemingly bleak openness and liminal feel.

So this is not a case of Northumbria's spirit fizzling out, but of extending along its eastern, marshy seaboard.

*(Sledmere, Fimber and the Wolds)*

## *Nature's Apprentice*

Mine was a feral childhood. Nature was in my DNA and I spent as much time as possible in the countryside around home, the dunes and beach, the peri-urban wastelands and fields, the local woodlands. My parents and older brother encouraged it and bent to my will in seeking out new wildlife experiences wherever we went.

Of all of these, perhaps the Yorkshire Wolds was the most important learning ground. We spent a couple of weeks or more and several weekends a year, at Sledmere at my Auntie Floss and Uncle Arthur's.

Sledmere is a one-off village, its smart arts and crafts buildings and its tall, farm walls painted a dark red and cream. It looks like a model village and it is a design extension of the Georgian Sledmere House, the seat of the Sykes family who own the whole place. My Uncle was Head Groom of the Sledmere racehorse stud, an integral part of the life of the village and Wolds.

Even today Sledmere is a backwater and largely unchanged, attracting visitors to its lovely house, gardens and curious war memorials. In the 1970s it was a rural idyll and the Wolds felt like the quintessential English countryside we read about in books like 'Cider with Rosie'.

David Hockney has captured, better than anyone, the essence of rolling, chalk fields and lines and clumps of ash trees which summarise The Wolds' character. To visit his exhibitions of almost life-size trees and Wolds' scenery, noting subtle changes through the seasons and years, makes me nostalgic for places which became part of me.

There is a built-in elegance and sparse beauty bordering on the brutal. Most of its fields are industrially cultivated, the soils being so fertile and well drained. The pastures are grazed to turf; these are the northern chalk downlands. The light, ploughed soils are spun through with white, like bits of land-bone.

Like all downland, it retains a framework of wildness. Tunnel-like lanes are barrelled by overhanging trees, while villages roll into the folds of dry valleys. Woodlands are planted on the tops of rounded hills as landscape gestures and, in field corners and combes, rarer flowers grow, supporting clouds of butterflies and other insects. From afar the whole landscape looks as if it is quietly rippling.

This partly manicured land is enhanced by its paddocks for thoroughbreds and, especially around Sledmere, tall, pointed 'monuments', which stand out above the trees. Among this were wildlife hotspots to be chanced upon.

Fimber Station, created as a personal station for the Sykes family in the 1880s, was a 'secret garden', an abandoned and ruined station house and waiting room, all the elements of a railway enthusiast's dream, the old platform and cutting half-colonised by scrub.

We ignored the signs and barbed wire and snuck in. It was a forgotten world, an excerpt from the 1940s, 'Adelstrop' grown over. We ventured upstairs on wafer thin boards, finding old metal signs for chicory coffee, OXO, Wills Whiffs and abandoned traps for moles, rats and birds, worm rotted tables and chairs.

It was here I felt, for the first time, the unrelenting power of Nature in winning back from people what had been taken from it. In about twenty years, the once, proudly maintained, country station had become re-vegetated. It was full of trees and bushes, elder and gorse, whin bushes, small ash and the odd apple and cherry tree, blackthorn and a self-seeded laburnum. It looked like wilderness in the making. Give it a few more years and you would struggle to find any hint of locomotion.

We watched a big rat swim back and forth across an open sewer. We saw bats flying up and down the old cut and we found chaffinch, song thrush and other birds' nests. Best of all were the stoats. Often we would see them cross the road as we travelled between Sledmere and Wetwang (to its great duck pond). They seemed to have adopted Fimber Station as their own.

Ginger hairstreaks with throat bibs the colour of farm butter, they entranced us with their chasing and curiosity. Always, when running past, they would turn, stop and look, sizing you up, fearless and ferocious to the last. The old station fair sang with mice, rabbits and the rats of course. It was a great place to be a stoat and a child.

Fimber Station, like many of my discoveries around The Wolds, was a little, intense world of living things, a sort of parallel universe of the wild, to be entered into, immersed in and closed behind you. It felt like the real world to me and something I knew I belonged in.

A little farther away was the old, chalk quarry and village tip, where once, whilst looking for fossils, my brother and I found an ancient tawny owl roost.

There were barrowfuls of pellets, coughed up over years, some of which had made a sort of compost of decayed fur and bone. I collected handfuls to analyse later and stuck the tiny red and yellow tipped teeth and jaws of shrews and voles to card.

Not all I learnt, as an under ten, in the countryside of Sledmere and The Wolds, was that exciting, but as a novice naturalist I had to learn everything and not just names, but the feel of places, habitats and fieldcraft.

I practised creeping up on and identifying common birds like mallard, finches, swallows and rabbits, where they all nested and fed, what preyed upon them. But they and the world they inhabited were exciting to me then. My Aunt's house had a field with bullocks at the back, with owls inhabiting old trees and even a bowling green and tennis court. The farther fields were edged by Horseshoe Wood and beyond that was Sledmere Castle, an abandoned shooting lodge, where I remember Dad pulling back the grass to reveal a pheasant, still sat on her nest.

The whole place was studded with these vignettes of wild encounter among a fun, recreational family life, a social as well as a wild landscape.

Perhaps more than anything was the implicit sense that everything in this Wold world, whether it was natural or man-made, was joined together and interdependent. As a boy, the fields and trees, wildlife and gardens, horse paddocks and farms, the people going about their daily lives, all seemed to be part of one continuous rhythm and coda. It was just how life should be. It was always a wrench to come back to the more complicated, modern life we led at home.

In recent times I've re-acquainted myself with Wold country and discovered rare Montagu's Harriers rising over fields near Kirby Grindlythe, red kites everywhere. I have walked the buried streets of abandoned, medieval village, Wharram Percy and watched again the barn owls in the same tree I first saw them in forty years ago, discovered the rich parklands, streams and meadows around Settington and Skagglethorpe, the trout infested waters at Wansford and the intriguing dry pastures and mini dales around Millington.

But those who personalised this place and gave it a human perspective have all gone now: Auntie Floss and Uncle Arthur, their lovely old neighbours Percy and Mary Hesp, Mrs Clarke at the Post Office, Mrs Beecroft at the shop, Bill Dillon in the gardens, Ben, the finger grabbing parrot. Even Fimber Station has been gentrified into a house and boring picnic site.

Time moves on. This is a place of memories and spent childhood, but still of deep connection. I will never lose my love of The Wolds, but there is sadness too. It is where I became apprenticed to Nature and experienced first-hand that it is not separate to us at all but part of every one of us.

You could also say I buried a piece of my heart in this part of Northumbrian countryside and I know I will always seek it out.

*(Goole, Blacktoft, York)*

# *Marshlands*

Flat and boring, even worse, wet, the flatlands and marshes around the Humber, in the southernmost reaches of the old Kingdom, are at first the least engaging and inspiring, especially if, like me, you are familiar with the obvious drama of the Northumbrian and Yorkshire coast and hills.

Perhaps you do really have to be born to the marshes to truly appreciate their subtle, wild beauty. But as you spend more time amongst them, their qualities grow on you. Their attraction lies in the edge-less-ness of reed and wetland habitats, stretching to the invisible and infinite horizon, under great savannah-like skies. Banks of cloud are reflected in their flat, still levels of pools, slowly moving waters and the changing light and wind movements on grass and reed.

As a child I spent hours watching birds in the remains of marshes around my home town of Marske by Sea, its name derived from the Saxon, 'Mersc', for marsh. I am familiar with the immersing qualities of reed beds and the excitement of being enclosed and hidden, sitting motionless, seeing the movements of sedge warblers and reed buntings close around me.

But here it is on a massive scale. Thousands of my local reed beds could be fitted into one corner of those I have discovered around the Humber and the Yorkshire peat-head levels, south of York, Doncaster and near Hull and Goole. Today, as impressive as they are, they are a fragment of what was once here.

This is the other face of Northumbria. It feels as if the energy of the hills and uplands has fully dissipated, finally rolling flat and dipping its geological toes to the sea. The atmosphere is different; it is open and raw, frameless and strangely liberating.

One late winter afternoon, in a bird hide at the Blacktoft Sands Nature Reserve, illustrates the haunting beauty of this area and the extent of its wildlife. The day fades and as it does, the light on the reedbed and pond, in front of us, rainbows from sky-blue to orange, the reeds becoming burnished gold, then gradually fading to light shades of violet and mauve. Through binoculars, a whole hide-full of people, thirty plus and me, scan the middle distance as one; we are here to witness a happening, a natural spectacle those in the know come to see time and again.

First one, then five or six at a time, big birds, raptors, come into view, hawking the marsh. They are marsh harriers returning from all over to their roost, after a day of hunting. There are ten and more now, circling, so distinctive on those long, thin wings and turning tails, glimpses of their owl-like faces staring back at us.

Then, one by one, neatly folding their angels' wings, suddenly collapsing, they parachute into the reeds, as if the reedbed had sucked them down, whole. Among the last to come in are two female and one male hen harriers, the females with their long ring-tails and white rump, the male all powder grey, ghost-like in the half light. These are the rarest raptors of all, on the brink of English, breeding extinction and we are especially lucky to see some of these survivors at their winter retreat.

I realise I have been holding my breath as I watch and I gasp out loud. I can hear sighs, coughs and whispers now, a sense of the show coming to the end, but a hush of reverence still hangs in the air. Many are still musing on how it must look in there, all those harriers, twenty seven counted and seen in just fifteen minutes, now at rest, folded into the reeds, just a couple of hundred feet away.

But then, as the colours fade to greys and browns, we look up as one; there is something bright white, floating along the hedge, behind the marsh and over it, a barn owl starting the night shift.

Walking slowly back in the dark, stark cold among the silhouettes of willows and reeds, people keep their peace and talk little, silenced by the experience. It feels like we have left a ritual, a spiritual undertaking, such a blessing it was to see the birds of the marsh drop into their reed-beds.

There is more, much more. The marshes give up their secrets willingly if you give them time. They draw your patience out, then offer up surprises. On a bright, June day I cycle through the lanes and fields around Swinefleet and almost fall off as a bittern flies up out of a drainage ditch to the side of me. The great, brown reed heron, flew over me so I could see every detail of this elusive bird, icon of marshes, normally so well camouflaged amongst its reedy haunt, where you are lucky to get a glimpse. In the full sunlight, it shines the colour of golden corn flecked with black and croaked loudly.

Other times I have been brought up fast by a flock of bearded reedlings. These exotic, long tailed, moustachioed titmice of the reeds look like no other English bird and their excited, energetic feeding and metallic calls bring a special energy to anywhere they appear.

The marshlands are a seemingly endless blank canvas, from which amazing things periodically emerge. They are the land of mists and mirrors, hiding and revealing in turn. It takes the magic of a Springwatch cameramen and the patience of Godot, to see into the intimate lives of birds like a bittern on the nest, harriers at rest, the habits of all the creatures that live amongst the stalks and waters. Just now and again we get a glimpse.

It's not just reedbeds either. Endless stands of umbellifore flowers, like hemlock and the purple angelica, nettles, grasses, sedges, meadowsweet and many more marsh plants, are home to as much life as the old, willow and poplar woodlands, rooted in wetland. These places are thick with warblers like whitethroat and sedge warbler and even the rare marsh and reed warbler. They are a metropolis for amphibians, fish and eels.

Howden Marsh is one such place. Howden is a village in the marsh and of the marsh. It retains its medieval character and its marsh, preserved as a local, nature reserve, sits on its outskirts. It is boardwalked and can be walked around easily, even at the wettest times, when the waters start to snake a little close for comfort to the houses. But what excitement to have such unspoilt, wild wetness so close. It reeks of ancient countryside with its veteran willows and poplar trees, its old embankments, its marshy, wet fields and ponds, a frog paradise. This is a taste of how it used to be to live in the marshes, a postcard piece, saved from the drains.

Further afield, near York, Yorkshire Wildlife Trust show me the wild side of York, Weldrake and the other 'Ings', acres of wet grass and marshy ground, periodically flooded and then dried out, seasonal wetlands good for flowers and birds. They are the product of luck and careful management, two sides of a coin, in winter, wet and covered in wildfowl, in summer thick, wet meadows. I can't believe I have never visited them until now.

Even more extensive are the Yorkshire and Humberhead Levels, mosaic mixtures of bog and marsh, covering miles of land at the head of the estuary, a place as much water as it is land. These are the lowland equivalents of the Pennine peatscapes and mires, reminders of Northumbria's water-world past.

I started by thinking of the marshlands of southern Northumbria as the poor relatives to the rest of the old, wild Kingdom. Not so, they are the keepers of secrets, flat and tome like, revealing by turns, their illuminated beauty as, page by page, we might turn and discover the animal imagery of the Lindisfarne Gospels or Book of Kells. For sure, these marshes hold part of Northumbria's old spirit in their reeds and waters.

*(Spurn Point and South Gare)*

# Spurned at Spurn

We were spurned at Spurn, oh yes. In the sea-watching bird hide, you could have heard a feather drop. We had misidentified a dot hovering over the rough sea, about a mile offshore. Shoulder to shoulder we sat, physically, but not in terms of expertise or status. Our neighbours were of a higher class of ornithologist it seemed and they felt it their duty to put us in our place.

Our crime, that day, was to mistake a Leach's petrel for a storm petrel. Well, it should have been obvious, of course, as it was pointed out, its 'hovering flight' was distinctive, but conditions were not great. Even in perfect light it would have been a challenge for most experts. Anyway, we stood corrected and left the hide suitably humiliated. Birding on Spurn, with its famous observatory and rarities so regular it attracts twitchers, birders and serious scientists alike, can be competitive as well as rewarding.

It is not just the birds and birders here that make Spurn special. It is its whole being. It has a bleak, wild edginess, borne of its nature, a long, thin spit of sand and gravel tormented by the North Sea, moving constantly and ever threatened with becoming a series of small islands.

Walking its windswept beaches you feel like you are teetering on the edge of the land, tolerated by the sea that could at any time take control. In this tenuous world there is nowhere to hide or retreat to.

Once, caught in a blast of a storm on the end, I cowered next to an old oil drum, as the sand and spume lifted around me and a flock of waders were flung past me, like so much buckshot. I felt then that there is something of the Armageddon about this place, a barrenness you might associate with catastrophe.

Recent storms have now actually ruined the only road and taken away much of Spurn's fragile infrastructure. Now, even more than before, it is of the sea, a natural, braided pier, extending into the seascape and poking it in the briny ribs. It is the sea's irritant. It spurns its advances but the sea is winning the war of attrition, surge by surge.

People have taken advantage of its unique position for thousands of years. In the muddy depths of its tides and in the sides of the Humber estuary nearby, have been found prehistoric boat yards and the remains of craft, launched on Bronze Age seas. They give us an insight into the first settlers' relationship with the water and land around the rivers, of the pre-Northumbrians.

For, in this 'land of six rivers' (the Forth, Tweed, Tyne, Wear, Tees and Humber) and via its many, smaller waterways, the first explorers and settlers, raiders and pioneers navigated far inland.

The temporal nature of Spurn provides a curious mix of human activity and interaction with natural forces. Birders are one expression of this. But so are the amazing array of war time bunkers and gun placements hidden in the dunes: the small lifeboat/coastguard peninsular community that live there: the people who visit to experience and be inspired by its wild beauty and its strangeness. Spurn is the sum of all these and many more parts.

It is one of the subtlest, wildest places and undeniably the eastern start and end of Northumbria, symbolic of the constant tussle between Nature and Humanity.

If Spurn is a part natural, part man-made spit of land-sea, then South Gare, the southern promontory of the Tees estuary, is a wholly man-made arm into the sea, with something of a similar character.

175

'The Gare' defies geology, its very make-up is invented. Built of clinker and slag, spewed out from the juxtaposed, iron and steel furnaces, since the late 19th Century, it has a wholly bleak beauty, comparable to Spurn and the much written about Dungeness, in Kent. There is a brutal mix of natural and human life down the Gare, a place of surprising juxtapositions.

In a scoop between sand dunes, are hidden a cluster of immaculate, green fishermen's huts. Bright coloured boats bob and sway in the tiny harbour of Paddy's Hole. Strange looking cabins have been forged of beach detritus, re-modelled vessels and industrial containers. There is an angry proclamation to return a stolen boat engine, tarred on the sea wall. This is a place that takes you on.

All this is happening against the backdrop of blast furnaces and coke ovens, clouded in gasps of sulphurous vapour. Woven into its slag fields, where the heat rises like a geothermal, are lagoons, dunes, ponds, reed beds and the fringes of the Tees estuary itself. Seals pass by, terns fly over, ships roll in and hares and owls race and glide in between. Migrant, vagrant birds are discovered like the rare wryneck (a Mediterranean woodpecker) I saw, sitting on a ball of slag, still warm enough to remind it of home.

There is more. Catch up with close-ups of purple sandpiper, their purple plumage and yellowlegs like vibrant jewels among the old gun mounts, off the end of the concrete peninsula. See the turnstones, all mottle backed and iridescent as oil, tracing round the ankles of fishermen who cast off the very tip under the squat, white lighthouse, dodging the seals. Gaze into a storm or bask in a day of complete stillness, as if becalmed on a sliver of land, quietly invited in, by the sea.

You could not make this place up and yet we did make it up.

Of all the places I have been in Northumbria, I have found nowhere wilder than the Gare or Spurn Point, their long, thin tendrils playing like wands with the winds and storms of the North Sea

*(Bempton and
Flamborough cliffs)*

# The YOC

Just how the Young Ornithologists Club became the repository for the most unruly and ill-disciplined, educational dropouts in school, escapes me. Perhaps it was because it was run by the well-intentioned RE teacher, Mr Tanoff, who was trying to calm them down or rehabilitate them, or was it just because they could get away with anything there?

Phil and I, a couple of years younger than the usually truant, chaos-causing, other members of the club, joined rather naively because we were interested in bird watching, something that didn't seem to feature highly on the agendas of 'Tex', the hapless leader of the gang or the other hooligans that surrounded us.

We also joined because the first trip out was to Bempton Cliffs, a spectacular nature reserve we had read about but never been to, a couple of hours away on the East Yorkshire coast. It was seabird city, a place of puffins and other exotic seabirds, nesting in their thousands in June.

The trip was certainly an education for us wide-eyed youths. The journey there was long remembered, it was so bizarre and awful. We embarked, sat facing one another, appropriately, Black Mariah style, and in what was more a van than a minibus, legs and feet alternating across the middle void, with bags and coats dumped underneath.

As Phil and I polished our binoculars, Tex brought out the first of several bottles of 'Newkie broon' from inside his parka pockets and the rest of the crowd started to consume them, ten minutes in. Tex was a rotund, heavy guy, with bonehead hair and grappling hands, not particularly aggressive, but seeming to lack any social niceties and prone to idiotic outbursts of loud laughter. He and his friends delighted in trying to wrestle, shaking the sides of the van, in their efforts. All seemed to excel, especially Tex, in loud and odorous emissions. The air became strongly tainted as we sat, mostly ignored, occasionally brought into the fray as props.

Things deteriorated quickly. All thoughts of birds retreated. Beer was spilt, slapstick was the order of the day, Rudie and Shaz snogged incessantly. Ashen-faced Sue slipped under our legs to the floor. Tex began to sing. Finally, when the fags were handed round, Mr T intervened, but by then it was a hopeless cause.

It was with immense relief that we arrived at our destination. Phil and I shot out of the van like buckshot and, while the rest twirled disorientated around the car park, we were off up to the cliffs, excited again at what we might see, fresh air and birds, the purpose of our quest remembered. That was the last we would see of Tex and gang for a while. They sat on the grass by the van in a huddle, looking tired.

From then on, the experience was on the up, Mr T came into his own, pinpointing and guiding us to all the best vantage points on these sheer, incredibly high, chalk cliffs. 'To think,' he said, 'that 'climmers' abseiled off these on old ropes to harvest the birds' eggs, right up to the 1950s'. We hoped Tex couldn't find any rope.

Puffins, puffins galore and up close. We couldn't believe their orange feet in real life and their rainbow bills. Guillemots, some bridled, their bills outlined in white, razorbills, kittiwakes, shags (you can imagine how they went down later). The place was alive with the birds we'd dreamed of. It was a sensual ambush, the sound of the cackling birds, the guano smell, the sheer numbers and breathless, unceasing activity of the colonies. Some larger ledges and outcrops were completely studded in birds, so that they merged into one seamless moving cacophony.

The gannet colony hammered it home. Massive, albatross-like birds with white, steel-stiff wings, tipped with black and soft, sulphur-yellow napes. They were beak-fencing, Bempton 'booby birds'. This was the only, mainland colony in the land, and they were almost close enough to touch. They even had young 'gulahs' which looked furry, not feathery, like reptilian penguins.

It went on and on, one natural surprise after another, eclipsing the awful journey. There was a cliff-top badger sett with heavy mounds of bright, red earth, dug out by the animals, right on the edge of the land. We planned to come back and watch them emerge, between sea and air.

We spied some 'rarities', to us anyway, a black redstart and a yellow wagtail, a peregrine flummoxing all the birds into a frenzy, as it circled out from its own nest, situated right amongst its potential prey.

These sights were amazing. But they were not, surprisingly, the most astonishing thing we saw that day at Bempton. The real eye-opener, the thing I will always remember, more than anything else, was something almost beyond belief.

Glancing across the gannet colony one last time, I caught the glint of glasses sparkling in the sun. It was coming from the other side of the gulley from where I stood. It was emanating from a person laid flat on their belly, gazing intently at the gannets through the biggest pair of eyeglasses I had ever seen. It was Tex. I watched him watching the birds, glued to the spectacle, captivated, silent and alone. I could not believe it.

The trip back was more subdued. Drink and excitement of one sort or another had taken its toll. But we did discover, between the snoring exchanges, the truth about Tex and the YOC and how his mates had come along for the ride, following their hero. No, they weren't interested in birds, but Tex was. It emerged that apart from beer, laughs and farts, Tex really loved birds. They talked to him in ways that teachers and people couldn't. He just enjoyed them and his mates accepted this, as one of his quirks. To this end he had 'borrowed' his Uncle's old seaman's binoculars for the outing and hidden them in his parka.

And so we learnt a lot that day. About birds, yes, but more importantly we learnt to never judge a bird book by its cover.

*(Near Malton, Woodbridge, and Boulby etc)*

## Boxers

*Running hare — red as a fox. Boulby — 7.9.14.*

As a northern naturalist, it has always been British mammals and birds that most excite me. I am mad about mustelids and have many memorable experiences of watching badgers, weasels, otters, stoats and even the occasional pine marten. Amongst my most frequent and delightful encounters are with hares. They thrive in the North East and Yorkshire in many habitats, whereas in other parts of England they are in decline.

On most walks I spot the distant shape of a hare, across a field or near a hedge, its ears peeping over the long grass. I have my eye tuned into their distinctive silhouette, the 'jizz and jazz', of hare.

Sometimes I am lucky to get up pretty close and, then, their intrinsic attractiveness comes alive: their size first of all, as big as cats and they even share some of the feline's elegant curves and movement and thick stroke-able fur, though they are primarily athletes, built for running: their piercing, amber eyes and characteristically large ears, tipped with black, diamond patterned and always moving. You can tell the mood of a hare by where its ears are at any one moment.

They often appear, without explanation and as if from nowhere. Tearing up the road, a young hare approaches, head on, and bolts past me, ears like blades, pared back, its whole being employed in the act of flight, a marathon runner intent on the finish line, or a fugitive in fear of its life. I turn my head to follow its course and as I do, it does a 'hand brake turn' to the left and ghosts under a gate, leaving no trace of its getaway or of ever existing.

Many people only see hares in spring, as they conduct their mad March antics, the females boxing at overenthusiastic and rival males, all chasing each other in drawn-out, spiralling, pushing matches. It's often the pure energy of the encounter that takes you aback, an expression of pure, hare life-force. It speeds your heart to watch them, their pugilist actions can be exciting, viscerally violent, and a little scary. It is Nature out of control. They could really hurt themselves! Fur flies.

I recall the thrill of watching up to five, embroiled in their mating ritual near Malton, on the edge of The Wolds, running between hedges and across undulating, agricultural land.

There is nothing gentle or restrained about it. They mean business, well-aimed punches to head and shoulders, mixed with flying kicks, the whole body jerking. It is mixed martial arts when hares fight.

Then there is a stand down, each poised, the air between them churning with menace, until they can contain themselves no longer and explode into a flailing mess again. Turning circles and sinuous eights, they pursue each other across and down the field, disappear for moments in the hedge, and then emerge hot and still angry.

The flow fight turns into a chase and ambush trial of fastest and fittest. More join in, three to five snaking along with the leader, often a female, twisting and turning to try and shake off its pursuers.

More fisticuffs follow and whittle the match down to two again, one obviously following the scent of the other's hindquarters, sensing breeding potential. But the doe is not in co-operative mood. This is a string along, a fight of elimination; the most agile buck gets to mate, but on her terms.

They are oblivious to outsiders and come up close, each by turns, trying to climb up and around the other, to subdue, smother by force, by whatever means.

They flow on and on, each individual a melt of movement and shape, a plasma of pelage, before disappearing as quickly as they appeared. With their angry delight dissipated, they slip off, soundlessly, into the ether.

This trick of coming out of nowhere and disappearing again is something hares share with roe deer and it gives them an understandable 'magical' quality. In folklore they are the familiars of witches, shape shifters and returning souls of the wronged dead, or fertility symbols.

They were also the traditional animal of Easter, before the bunny. At the Pagan festival of Eostr, at the vernal equinox, hares were the sacred animal of the Teutonic goddess of Dawn. Celts would not eat them, despite their long pursuit for coursing and game. There is something other-worldly about every encounter with a hare.

Hares are the embodiment of energy and have adapted to niches across Northumbria, from fields and grasslands to woods and moors. Yet they may not even be native and are often cited as being introduced here in the Iron Age. This appears confounded by their presence at the famous Mesolithic site at Star Carr, near Scarborough, though it is possible these were mountain hares, still about from the post glacial phase.

They certainly belong here now, indigenous or not, like the people from many cultures, that came in waves, across the centuries and became part of and shaped this place. Fast and furious, slightly mysterious, they are the blade-running beauties that weave their running patterns, around our lives and lands.

*(Skipsea, Hornsea, Holderness
and near Scarborough)*

# Eden

Mr Moo's ice-cream parlour, off the coast road near Bridlington, in the wide, open fields of Holderness, is a good place to stop for a break and a delicious way of making a discovery about the ancient wildlife and landscape history of southern Northumbria. You can even stay at the beaver dam campsite.

"Beaver dam", I hear you say, "What's that got to do with ice cream?" To find out, take the mile-long path between thick hedgerows and newly-planted trees from Mr Moo's, passing also the dairy cows so important to our enjoyment, and you will end up on a rocky beach with your back to the famously fast eroding, boulder clay cliffs behind you. Turn slowly around and the mystery is revealed. Stuffed into a wide section of the clay are thousands of old tree trunks and branches, tightly packed and jumbled up together, a mass of sticks and tree limbs, from top to bottom of the fifteen foot cliff and extending sideways over about thirty feet.

It looks, at first sight, as if a massive log jam has been fossilised and enclosed into the clay and is being slowly exposed. That is exactly what it is happening. The layers of wood were first seen in 1996 and have gradually become more and more obvious. Archaeologists puzzled over the deposits. Could it be a wooded causeway or platform deliberately conceived by early man?

They did find some flint arrowheads in it, dating to the early Neolithic Stone Age (which might better have been called the wood age, its use was so prolific, but not preserved). Close examination revealed a mixture of ash, oak and alder and that some of the trees had been chiselled by beavers. They concluded that, at the very least, the wooded layer was the outer edge of a big beaver dam, or a number of them, reconstituted and mixed together as a flood deposit. That parts of the woodland floor and smaller parts of the wooded environment were also preserved probably meant it had not moved far.

A 5000 year old beaver dam eroding out of the cliff is an exciting prospect for those of us interested in the ancient, wild environs of our landscape and ancestors. Standing there, I started to see for myself the evidence everywhere of gnawing and chewing and was even able to pick out hazelnuts, one or two of which had been nibbled by prehistoric wood mice. That is what I call 'time travel'.

Recent evidence shows beavers thrived in Northumbrian wetlands at least until the 14th Century, they are part of our landscape heritage and places like Beverley, are named after them.

The Mr Moo, sorry, the 'Withow Gap beaver dam', affords a much broader insight even than that of the dam itself; it offers a way into understanding the significance of this flatland area of south Northumbrian landscape, from the Vales of York and Pickering to the Holderness and lower Humberside coast and even the north coast of Northumberland and coastal estuaries, all part of similar environs about the same time.

 Indeed it didn't stop there. In earlier times the North Sea was non-existent. The marshes, wetlands and islands extended across to hills now buried under the sea, which archaeologists call 'Doggerland' after the undersea Dogger Bank, a submerged part of Northumbrian upland, inundated when England became separated from the continent, about 10,000 years ago.

This Lakeland history resonates with the other, lost water bodies that were once present much farther north from Prestwick Carr, near

Newcastle airport, to the Morebattle border, lost lakes and many more besides. Northumbria has long been a land of both wetlands and uplands, contrasting one with the other.

There are other clues too. A few miles south of Scarborough lies Star Carr. Today it is an almost featureless, productive, agricultural land, made up of big, arable fields, straggly hedgerows, wet meadows and thorn scrub, a bit overworked and industrialised. Beneath, it is peaty and in places waterlogged. 'The Carrs' is a damp area between the moors and Wolds, hinting at its wetter past.

A once extensive lake did exist here, one of several in the area, formed after the glacial retreat of the last Ice Age, including the massive Lake Pickering. Star Carr was on former Lake Flixton. Eleven to nine thousand years ago, it was a lake with islands and a fringe of reed, swamp, alder and willow wet woodland and ringed by extensive 'wildwood'.

It may seem a bit scruffy and unremarkable today, but back then you would have been staring into 'Eden'.

We are used to talking about the decline in biodiversity over the last fifty or hundred years and it is true, we are impoverished, even by recent, historical standards. Just hundreds of years back, all of the big animals, naturally found in the UK, were long gone and the countryside was anything but natural.

Was there ever a time that wildlife and people lived in balance and harmony, where the ecosystems were in peak presence?

Yes. That time of near paradise, for people and animals in the North Eastern UK, was between about ten and five thousand years ago and the excavations of the fields about Star Carr and beyond, like the beaver dam, have revealed how this was a time of special abundance. From Scarborough to Bridlington and the Humber, this land was rich in natural resources. These peats, over fifty years of analysis, have revealed every part of our mega-fauna as well as the things we are more used to today. Brown bear, wild boar, wild cattle, elk, beaver, lynx and wolf lived alongside otter, wild cat, fox, red and roe deer, badger, hare and hedgehog and many bird species, some, like crane and stork, as common then, as they are rare today. In the earliest layers are impressive footprints of wild horse.

The people who hunted, gathered and settled on the sides of these lakes, built lakeside platforms to hunt and fish from, made camps they lived in most of the year and lived off biodiverse land, in the days before farming.

They did not apparently take all this for granted. Their elders would have told tales of the ancestors and their living memory of suffering through much harsher times, when the climate was freezing and unforgiving, the game harder to find and get close to. They lived now in good times, it was paradise to them. Marking this, they ritualised the abundant, natural order, taking the red deer as a totem animal, wearing ceremonial headgear made of their antlers and skulls and making offerings to the lake, to thank it for their rich harvest.

It sounds like a script from a movie doesn't it? A sort of caveman Nirvana, though these people lived in huts not caves. Every part of what I describe here, is evidenced by the many finds from Star Carr and other related sites, with only a bit of personal embroidery. You will have to visit the Yorkshire Museum in York to see for yourself and make up your own mind if it really was Heaven on Earth.

With the wildlife tick-list that existed then, it definitely would have been for me, even if there wasn't any anaesthetic or antibiotics. Call me nostalgic and idealistic, craving for times of near perfection, I confess I would like to be zapped back, for just a short time at least, to experience life when we were just another creature in the swamps, woods and hills.

Luckily, I think that is what we can get a little of, in the wilds of Northumbria, even today. Maybe not so dramatic and dangerous or diverse, but there are reminders of these and later periods too, everywhere we look. We still see places full of wildlife, it's all relative. We can experience, at least in microcosm, the wet woods and marshes ancient people inhabited, such as in my now, frequent trips to the Humberhead levels.

But you can't beat a good 'carr', a lovely alder or willow wet woodland. I found myself in one on the edge of The Moors. It was a tiny corner of mature alder, a fragment of boggy ground in the bend of a river. The trees were great, old specimens, tall and thick-trunked, bifurcating wildly, their roots partially exposed, reminiscent of mangrove swamp.

What drew me to stand in their damp shade, was that the largest specimens seemed to form a distinct circle, several metres across. I stood in the middle of them, a wet, grassy hollow and realised that they did indeed form a natural growth circle and that all of the trees, though appearing single, were in fact formed of the same tree; they were mature, coppice trees, connected underneath, the original middle long rotted away.

This was a very old ring of trees, or single tree, I had stumbled upon. Stunned by this, I thought this was just the sort of 'natural magic' that would appeal to our forebears, a living, natural, wood circle, perhaps a forerunner of, or inspiration for the henges, wood and stone circles we went on to build.

There is even a real remnant of the lakeside living of the Mesolithic on our doorstep, at humble Hornsea Mere, the biggest natural lake in Yorkshire. At about two miles long and one wide, it is the last remainder of those glacial lakes of the flatlands south of Scarborough. Back then there were about seventy or more hereabouts alone.

Hornsea Mere is a pleasant place to walk, boat, watch birds and even buy local pottery, the local clays we saw on the coast being put to good use. I have visited it on and off for years and watched wildfowl and passerines there, with semi–rarities like yellow-browed and icterine warbler and black tern, turning up regularly.

It is its fringe of willow carr and reeds I like the most. They are small and sparse, compared to those on the Humber estuary, but nowhere else do you quite get the sense of being in the reeds around an ancient lake. Only the Northumberland loughs come close, but they have a colder, upland atmosphere.

Standing there, with my telescope and tripod slung over my shoulder, I can feel, just for a moment, like one of those hunter gatherer 'Adams', concealed in the reeds and ready to take from my natural larder, returning later that day to my 'Eve', not in my Skoda Roomster, but weaving my way through the creeks, following the paths of animals to our camp on the side of a bigger lake, a few miles away.

There is hope yet for my flight of fancy. The Carrs Wetland Project aims to re-wet and diversify parts of the Vale of Pickering and return it to a more natural balance. Elsewhere, as at Prestwick and in the Sedgefield Carrs, there are similar, re-wilding initiatives.

Wouldn't it be great if we could reconstruct just a part of our wetland past by conserving, connecting and restoring some of the wildlife rich, marsh and carr landscapes, across Northumbria, a taste of the lost Northumbrian Eden?

*To the **Ends** of it all, forays into outposts of Northumbria*

# *Edge-lands*

Where to draw the line? My mind map of the North defies even the greatest extent of Northumbria, pushing beyond boundaries, within reason. I have collected landscape experiences and wild encounters from just beyond but where I still sense a connection, in spirit, landform, habitat or culture. So I crept into Cumbria and recalled my student days, mapping in the Lake District. This area was never totally Northumbrian; it was an annexe allowed to rule itself.

Likewise, Ingleton, the foundation experience of my love for waterfalls across Northumbria, lies between south Cumbria and the Forest of Bowland, in the Yorkshire Dales, just about in the boundary. Bowland, itself, that undiscovered corner, was part of the western extension of Northumbria. Merseyside was, at first, a landscape too far west to feel Northumbrian, but has such special, wild, dune habitats I had to include it in my edge zone.

Finally, the incredible landscape of 'The Roaches', in the Staffordshire part of the White Peak, cannot be missed. This landscape is northern in character, big and jagged and of Pennine grit, geologically akin. It also has a deep mythology and folk lore, with everyone from King Arthur to Robin Hood featured in its hills and woods. It seemed to embody much of the spiritual essence I associate with Northumbrian classic landscapes, like the Sandstone Hills of Northumberland and the moors of Pennine Durham, Tees and Yorkshire.

It is as if the qualities that are contained in the landscapes of the North East can be picked up almost anywhere, a reflection of how we feel and approach a place.

There is a bit of Northumbria in most of our English landscapes, just as there is 3-4% of Neanderthal, the original 'wild man and woman', in all of us.

Being 'Northumbrian' is then a state of mind, linked to a sense of wild Nature, helped along by local, landscape character.

*(Ingleton, Roughting Linn, High force,*
*Dudshager and near Moorsholm)*

# The Falls

Waterfalls are hypnotic. We are affected by their force, marvelling at their power and beauty. The sheer scale and majesty of Niagara, Victoria and other, great falls around the world have a sacred draw. Those closer to home are not so immense or always revered, but are as impressive in their own way. I, long ago, fell under their spell.

As a young boy into Tarzan, waterfalls held a special excitement, as I pictured myself being able to dive off them, ape-man style, and hide in secret caves behind them. Nowhere did this come more to life than at Ingleton Falls in the Yorkshire Dales. The waterfall walk is somewhere I return to regularly.

Just under five miles long, it is a horseshoe-shaped trail, up the river Twiss and down the river Doe, linked, at the top by farmland. Along its length are a series of nine main and many smaller waterfalls, revealed in sequence, as you pass through ancient, oak woodland and the edge of the moor. They range from long and turbulent rapids, to sudden-drop cascades. Their names give a clue to their form, such as Pecca Twin Falls, Hollybush Spout, Thornton Force, Triple Spout and Snow Falls.

The falls have been a modest, tourist attraction since the late Victorian era and being on privately owned land, you pay an entrance fee, which today is a quite hefty £6. That their natural spectacle has been traded on, speaks of being part of the Victorian-Edwardian revival of the 'come and see' Romantic Picturesque tradition. The idea was to exhibit the best features Nature has to offer, as a demonstration of pure, wild beauty. Looking at them now, you can see why. They are definitely 'worth it'.

A further demonstration of their value, is that it has long been the tradition to throw a coin into their pools to make a wish, a watered down ritual that echoes prehistoric practices. Near the entrance to the trail, at Swilla Glen, is a dead tree, probably an oak, but it is difficult to tell, as it is completely covered in coinage. Coins from the 1970s onwards, perhaps some earlier, have been pushed into its bark, so that it has become metalled along its whole length. There are others like it in parts of North Yorkshire and Scotland, 'wishing trees', perhaps started as an alternative to throwing offerings into the falls; at least, you could see where your money was going!

I recall dragging myself up the hill toward the moor in my new monkey boots, crossing shale tips from old lead mines and stopping for a picnic at the top. It was the early 70s and a Polaroid of the family shows Dad with a crew-cut and orange jumper and my Mam wearing a brightly patterned dress and easy shoes, carrying a large, glitzy handbag. It was, after all, a day out.

One of the highlights for my brother and me, was stopping at Twistleton Farm, at the head of the valley, where you could get milk 'straight from the cow'. The milk and the milkiness of the waters below will always be associated in our minds with this place.

The first of the falls sounded and flowed into view through the trees. Pecca and Pecca Twin Falls were impressive enough, substantial curtains of thick, white waters and turbulent flow. Hollybush Spout was a taller, thinner affair. Glimpses of wagtails, dippers and even red squirrels kept you on the lookout and excited.

All this was preparation towards what, to me and even Wordsworth, who also visited, was and is the most dramatic of all, Thornton Force. This fifty feet high fall is really big by UK standards and seems to hold a lot of water, its shape straight from a textbook. It is formed by an unusual, geological feature and the resulting, hard rock ledge, over which water flows, overhangs away from the cliff, where softer rocks are scooped out from under it, forming a shallow cave.

This means that, in most conditions, you can actually walk behind the water and crouch on a ledge, gazing through the thick surge, Tarzan style. I can still feel the excitement of the first time, really being in the flow, suffused in its ozone vapours, gradually soaked by its dewed droplets, a sensuous treat.

Across Northumbria, waterfalls are a recurring point of interest, marking where uplands tumble into valleys, step by step, from moor to sea. Cauldron Snout is the longest, but is really a cataract of churning waters, partly tamed by the Cow Green Reservoir. Downstream, High Force is a true beauty, a calendar fall and at 71 feet, one of the tallest in England. Standing on top, close to its lip, you can sense the vertigo of its sheer drop to the plunge pool below, where the Rayban sunglasses, which fell from my head as I peered too close, thirty years ago, probably still reside.

Apart from Ingleton, I have two, enduring favourite falls that are especially inspiring. One is in Northumberland and the other in East Cleveland, just off the North York Moors.

Roughting Linn is famed for its great panels of prehistoric rock art, like at Old Bewick, but even more so. They were picked into the sloping side of a whaleback of gritstone near Wooler. Early Stone Age in origin, they form a series of complex rings and cup marks, some showing several, concentric, grooved rings around a central cup and there are channel and tail-like marks and even, in one place, what looks like a sort of faucet, carved into the rock, similar to those at Ilkley and nearby at Old Bewick.

Whatever their original significance and meaning, people today often decorate them and leave offerings. Over the years I have seen sweets, flower petals, berries and ribbons added to highlight their features. It is still a place of gentle ritual, probably designed for that purpose by our Northumbrian, ancestral aborigines.

As a whole, especially in the rain, many have noted how they resemble and facilitate flowing water, the patterns imitating pools and eddies, the concentric shapes of raindrops. Some even venture to describe them as 'kinetic water features' designed to come to life in heavy rainfall and 'capture' the energy of life giving water*.

So it may be no coincidence then that 'linn' means waterfall in old Northumbrian, and that, close by the carved rock outcrop, is the waterfall of Roughting Linn, after which it is named. Climb down here and some of the possible, past, ritual and sacred meaning of the carvings become amplified. It is a natural, intimate amphitheatre, with powerful, flowing water as its focus. The atmosphere

is serene, utterly peaceful and still, but for the sound of water.

I have seen similar associations between rock art and waterfalls from Ilkley to Western Scotland and it puts me in mind of the largest falls I have ever seen, at Dudhsagar, in southern India's Western Ghats. Deep in the jungle, we emerged to see enormous, tiered falls, hurtling down the mountain side, the plunge pool of cold waters filled with women in their saris taking the waters, monkeys running in the trees above them. Natural features like this are seen in India as life-giving and are ritualised. People bathe and leave offerings, mark them in different ways.

Likewise, here in Northumbria, water, the key to survival and symbol of life itself, its lifeblood, has always been written throughout its rocks, waterways and wetlands.

One more fall to visit. This one is off limits though. It lies in a deep, wooded cleft near the village of Moorsholm, off the radar. It is not shown on the map. Only one photograph exists so far on the internet, standing in frozen flow, in the hard winter of 1982 and it is unnamed. It was found by accident, a serendipitous fall.

At thirty feet tall, it is as impressive as some of the Ingleton examples. Tall enough for Tarzan. Somehow its mystique adds to the thrill of visiting it, always being careful that no one is watching. It is hard to get close to, but you can scramble down the bank and secrete yourself into its rocky sides, gaze up at its cold, clean, vertical waters which tumble between trees.

Closing my eyes, I am enveloped by the relentless crash of water and included in its flow. In this immersed state, I begin to picture the rivers, streams, becks, cleughs, burns, ghylls, denes, howles, drains and dykes, all flowing at this very moment from source to sea: the circulatory system of Northumbria. It is all these waters that lace together everything that lives in and upon this land.

*See reading list, Brian A Smith

*(Forest of Bowland, Langholm)*

# The Bowland Harriers

They are often nicknamed, 'sky dancers', as the flight of the hen harrier is surprisingly light and floating, for a big bird of prey. These are gracile birds, thin, long winged and tailed, economic in every movement. To watch one, quarter a bog or moor, is to witness a moving brown or grey shuttlecock, propelled, it seems, by the whim of wind and air alone: glide, hover, float, sink backwards into backdraft, stutter back, then forwards, hanging low, then higher, suddenly beating off in a direct line, heading into the haze of summer. Wings held almost flat and then shallow v-shaped, long tail turning like a rudder, this is the flight of the hen harrier.

All along, watching through binoculars, you are aware of the binocular stare coming back at you, the radial mask with large, deep, embedded eyes, more owl than hawk, focussed on anything that moves, fur or feather. Then the trailing talons grab and hold their package of takeaway food, eaten nearby, in the deep grass or heather, or carried back for hungry chicks.

Their plumage also sets them apart, not the most colourful, yet elegant and arresting, all the same. The female is speckled, barred brown and often has a distinctive, ringed tail, but the male is one of the most stunning of all British birds, in its grey, almost chalky blue garb, which gives it a phantom-like quality.

They congregate in quite some numbers in their winter roost sites, such as the big bogs of Tregarron in mid Wales, or the Norfolk marshes, where they join their more localised marsh cousins. In Scotland too, they are regularly seen but uncommon, places such as Mull being good at all times of year.

Just over the Newcastleton Hills, in the edges of the Borders, on Langholm Moor, they nest colonially, a loose group of up to eight pairs raising double figures of young. This is the result of an enlightened experiment, where they are tolerated and managed, given diversionary food to stop them taking too many grouse, highly prized game birds.

It works to a degree. In England no such approach has yet been taken and as a result so near, yet so far away, we have few if any nesting hen harriers; they are nearly extinct as breeders in this country. There isn't much physical difference between the moors of The Borders and Northumberland or Yorkshire, but there is in human attitude it seems. The English hen harrier has been singled out and secretly persecuted, almost out of existence by those intent on maximising the numbers of grouse bagged for elite entertainment and profit, it is claimed.

The hen harrier is the conservation bird of the moment in this, the second decade of the 21st Century. The long-held zero tolerance of harriers by some moorland owners and keepers, is now actively being challenged. A minority of these employ illegal methods to remove, kill or disturb their nesting in some form of misconstrued attitude, inherited from Victorian times. Yes, harriers do take grouse and can impact on the numbers that can then be shot and killed by highly paying guns. But these are protected birds and they were here first, their survival should not be at the behest of commercial sports interests, however influential. It is strange that they are vilified and hated to the degree they have been.

It can get very nasty. Whilst most people are amazed by the flight of the hen harrier, this is not shared by all. It is hard to get into the mind-set of the keeper who, reportedly, on being shown a nest full of gorgeous, young harriers, by a delighted under-keeper, smashed and stamped them to bits in front of him. Such violence and anger is deep set and disturbing.

The field is changing; everyone is at least talking about the issue and a Hen Harrier Joint Recovery Plan has been written, though not published so far, as no-one can agree finally on its measures. There are calls to licence moorland grouse shoots and to stop certain forms of highly disturbing, driven shoots and to manage grouse for quality not quantity.

Moorland managers, in more tolerant mood, suggest that up to three pairs of harriers could be accepted on a moor, but that the third or even second and third pair could then be repatriated, down south, to a non-grouse moor, like Dartmoor, by taking their young into captivity. That it should come to this now seems sad at best. Surely the rare harriers should come first, especially when just over the border, at Langholm, they are showing how it could be done, though shooters will need to compromise.

To see a hen harrier in its breeding finery in Northumbria today, you will have to go from one extreme or the other. Langholm is probably your best bet, but Scotland as a whole is quite good. Tracking down an English harrier is almost impossible, but a pair bred in the Peaks in 2014 for the first time in years, the 'peaky blinders'! They try now and again and did breed, in single numbers, in Northumberland, in the 1990s briefly but have not succeeded for some time, always being 'put off'.

Only one place was, until recently, guaranteed. This was in a far, western outpost of the old Kingdom, between Lancashire, the Dales and Pennines, the Forest of Bowland. This pretty, undiscovered area has quiet vales, hills, woods and moorlands owned, not entirely by grouse shoot interests, but also by private utility companies. They have been the last bastion of hen harriers in England, though even there, nesting is now ad hoc.

I remember the thrill of walking in to try and see them, following the wall-lined, valley paths and sparse topped sycamores, then making our way onto the rough moors, that could have been anywhere in the Pennines or North Yorkshire, except they had not been burnt to encourage new heather to feed grouse and there was more tree scrub.

We got distant, but good views, like those described at the start: a female ringtail, briefly off the nest and an almost silver male, patrolling his territory. There was no sense of fear that, at any moment, a hidden gun would pop up and take them out, or some psychotic keeper would mangle their young in the adults' absence, or set the moor alight to destroy the birds. It was a well-protected site too, a 24 hour watch was being kept on the nest site. We could just delight in their sky-dancing antics.

I am, though, optimistic about the harriers in England, as well as elsewhere. The arguments now fully raised in the open, are being worked out and the lessons of Langholm and efforts of more enlightened, moorland owners and managers, will ensure the grouse economy keeps going, alongside a healthy population of hen harriers and other rare birds.

Even those few, violent individuals, with no respect for wildlife, or anyone, will be bred out. As the state of Nature gets more critical, intolerance of rare and beautiful species like the hen harrier, will be even less accepted or tolerated by society. The hen harrier then will be a more common sight.

When that day comes, another fragment of wildness will have been restored to our Northumbrian landscape heritage. I will dance to that!

*(Skelghyll and Wansfell and the Hundreds,
Troutbeck Bridge, Cumbria)*

# *Skelgyhyll*

If you have to go you've got to go! In the great outdoors there are no toilets. But it doesn't have to be embarrassing or uncomfortable, you just have to choose your place and thick moss nearby helps too.

Of all the places I've 'been' in the countryside, Skelghyll set the standard early on, on the bog bush front, where in comfort and drama I hung over the precipice of the steep-sided, Lakeland gulley, nested in the tree canopy, on my natural, Y-shaped branch, toilet seat.

Nineteen and alone in the hills, undertaking my university, geological mapping project, I was often in need of a place to hang out, to recover from a beer-induced, dodgy stomach.

It was a good place to contemplate too, truly beautiful, dangling there, listening to the tinkling stream, a hundred foot below in the oak, alder and rowan-filled ghyll. Luckily for my embarrassment, I never saw another soul, my toilet and thoughts were undisturbed, bare arsed and suspended, in relief.

I could have sat there all morning, slightly moving in the breeze, musing to myself in the dappled sunlight, but I had another job to do. I had fossils to find, identify, to pin down and rock sequences to plot on my emergent, geological map.

So I pulled up my pants, took my head out of the clouds and wandered down to the streamside, walking along until I found a likely exposure, a handy outcrop, to examine.

Skeghyll is still an amazing place in many ways, not just for its handy, natural conveniences, more because it feels cocooned, undiscovered and genuinely unspoilt and yet it is a spit from the tourist focus of Ambleside, rising behind the Waterside Hotel.

It was so green and bright then, so leafy and sunny, that looking back it is like a Greek grove bathed in an amber glow, the stumbling brook in its deep cleavage, a copper-gold sheen, in which I stood, ankle deep, reading the rocks.

This is a famous place for geologists, a spot for finding some of the most ancient, yet curiously misunderstood critters of all time, 'the graptolites'. I was intrigued by them, as no one knew what they were. In the hand they looked like fancy eye lashes, scribed into the dark, fine shales. Curved, straight, convoluted branchlets, an inch or so long, preserved in fools' gold, with tiny segments and burrs, or 'thecae', they looked every bit like elegant, miniature, life forms.

They were easy to find once you got the right horizon; the rocks were stuffed with little Silurian bodies that filled the dark, silty seas, 380 million years ago.

Their names were also historic, recognised as some of the first zone fossils that could accurately date mini epochs, by their relative abundance in time and specificity. They were named after the geologists who discovered their bespoke significance and particular morphology. Hence, Monograptus Sedgewicki, the namesake of the Victorian rock man, Sedgwick, and names descriptive of their diverse shapes, from the single branched mono and double branched dimorphograptus, to the circular spirograptus.

Evocative names indeed then, for these subtle but intriguing impressions of an ancient diluvian mystery. Were they single animals in themselves, the debate ran, or parts of a bigger, more complex creature, so far undiscovered, or mere antennae, mouthparts, legs or feelers?

No one knew and I liked them all the more for their mystery. I filled my rucksack with them, wrapped them carefully in the toilet tissue I had not wasted earlier and tramped off back to the tent to lay them out on a picnic table display, before my afternoon doze. I had to be careful not to overexert myself; I had growing to do, I needed my rest and the pub would be open soon.

I vividly remember one night, after a pint or two, pondering on the graptolite question, among other things, with my head stuck out of the tent, lying on my back and looking up at a perfect night sky.

I watched the most miraculous meteor shower I've ever seen. Even now, years later, it has no equal: constant flashes over the whole sky, all night long, a retinal picture etched into my memory forever. Sleep would not come, with the night so alight.

What was a graptolite really, an alien life form? What if one is still alive somewhere in some deep sea, lying undiscovered? If the stars could do this, I decided, anything was possible.

Years later they found the answer. My old geology Professor, Dick Aldridge and colleagues, found they were linked organisms, sharing the same skeleton, floating on the surface of Silurian seas. It was part of his life's mission and scientific legacy.

But, for me, the upshot of this is that we are no better off for knowing. It is not the finding out, but the not knowing that is most exciting, being kept guessing.

The contemplation of truths and untruths, of life's mysteries, that is what makes things interesting. How boring it would be if, in moments of ablutionary bliss, or just lying about watching the night sky, all the answers were immediately at hand. Life and mystery need time, to unfold and grow, if they are to be true revelations.

*(Sefton Coast)*

# Merseysiders

I must admit, I find it hard to envisage a Northumbrian speaking with a scouse accent. But the old maps, showing the full extent of ancient Northumbria, do show it extending into Merseyside, via the Wirral, to Mersey Bay. This was a western extreme of Celtic Christian influence and authority, a constituent part of the whole.

As far as being part of a zone of Northumbrian landscape and natural history, it brings an extra element of excitement and reinforces the importance of dunes, which are a feature, right down the East coast.

Those around Sefton and Formby, on the north Mersey estuary, eclipse all others, in the range of species they support. For this reason alone, it seems a good idea to include this western outpost of the natural and Celtic Kingdoms in my overview. I'm going with the natural accent of the land.

Sand dunes are brilliant. I grew up playing in them, catching common lizards (alas not that common then and even less so now), counting the plants and butterflies, a rich herbage of plants good at soaking up and maintaining the little water that stays on them, amongst which, the lizards and other creatures thrived.

On Druridge Bay and at Embleton, on the Northumberland coast, on Holy Island and Ross Links and Bamburgh, on the Redcar coast and Tees estuary, on the East Yorkshire coast including Spurn, the dunes extend for miles and get to some heights, supporting linear plains of marram grass and florally rich turf communities. In the wetter areas, in their slacks, they have ponds and wet grasslands that are favoured by amphibians. Owls and kestrels hunt among them and skylarks rise above and nest there.

Dunes are the last line of defence from the sea, along the lower parts of the coast without cliffs to protect them; they form a fringe of spikiness and crusty, moving sands which frame the coast.

On the Sefton seaboard, behind conifer plantations, that also have some of the best and most accessible, surviving red squirrel populations in the North of England, lie the extensive Ainsdale dunes. These, the lagoons and the soggy, boggy habitat mosaics behind them, are home to the rarest of amphibians and reptiles.

Several times, over the years, I have ended up on this coastal strip, an unlikely nature reserve of such importance. It is just up the road from the Liverpool conurbation and its beaches, which can seem bleak and urbanised and are driven on by cars, trampled by thousands, so that fences have had to be erected, to protect the best bits.

It has a feeling of an industrial estuary on a scale bigger than even the Tees. It also shares something of the untamed wildness, that peculiar mix of human and natural conditions we find at South Gare and Spurn; it seems an 'unadopted' land.

Close by are the gardens of the upper-middle class urbanites, seeking homes away from but near the city, with a spattering of famous footballers' massive homesteads. The red squirrels are very much at home here too, feeding off millionaires' bird tables. It is a place of such contrasts.

The dune slacks, which are of central interest and the reason I come here, are not outwardly dramatic at all. But they are where the rare ones roam.

I always get shown around these protected areas by the Sefton Ranger Service, who know its details and subtleties. In spring the ponds are alive with breeding amphibians, common frogs, toads and newts in the deeper areas, including the great-crested and palmate varieties. But look closer and in some there is a different sort of toad, a slimmer, more pointed one, with a golden stripe down its back; this is the rare natterjack toad, only found here and on one or two other parts of the south coast.

One year, I was slightly later visiting and I came across ponds full of the tiny offspring of the natterjack, the size of a finger nail. Tiny beauties swirled in the pond edges into the night, as adults made their distinctive, high pitched croaks, the loudest amphibians in Europe.

There is another surprise here, but harder to find. This is the sand lizard, our only, egg-laying lizard and a jewelled spectacle of a reptile, bigger, bolder and a lot more glitzy than the humble but also gorgeous, common or viviparous lizard, which gives birth to live young.

Sand lizards, like the natterjack, are sand burrowers and make a breeding tunnel, in which they lay their eggs. The males are territorial and their shining, emerald colours are aimed at display and warding off rivals, the peacocks of the British, herpetological world.

The common lizard is local but ubiquitous, found on most dune systems, whilst the sand lizard is a rarity, only found normally on the south coast in very few areas, but both are widespread on the continent. It is interesting to note the cold and exposed abode, afforded by the Mersey estuary for its rare creatures, in contrast with that of their softer brethren in the south. These Merseyside toads and lizards are well hard.

What they have in common it seems, is just the basic, dune slack habitats. By some Northumbrian accident, remainder populations of these rarities have survived in isolation, marooned 'up North'.

There are other rarities here too, with over thirty, uncommon plants, such as the petalwort that likes dynamic, disturbed dunes, and orchids of many varieties, including the dune helleborine. Rarer birds, like the black-tailed godwit and knot inhabit the beaches nearby, dabbling among the strange sculptures of Liverpudlians, marooned in the incoming tide.

But is this still wild Northumbria?

Roaming in the dunes, my damp trousers tucked into soaked socks, in saturated boots, bowed by a sharp, cold wind off the Irish Sea and examining tiny natterjacks, in freezing hands, treading carefully around the islands of turf communities, to avoid sleepy, emerald lizards, it feels wild and Northumbrian enough for me.

*(The Roaches,
Staffordshire Peaks)*

# The Hen Cloud

The name of this great hill sounds Native American to me and I find myself, as I approach its steep slopes, reciting under my breath the rhythmic sounds of all the tribes I can recall. They merge into a sort of chant, marking my upward progress. 'Navaho, Pawnee, Cheyenne, Cherokee, Shawnee, Arapaho, Comanche, Shoshone, Wichita, Chinokan, Apache, Cree, Hopi, Sioux.' I enjoy the feel of their quiet pronunciation, my mouth rounding over soft tones. It also distracts me from the ascent, which today is laborious, weighed down by aching hips.

But I am not in Nevada or Wyoming, but in the Staffordshire Peak District, the White Peak, and a geomorphological leftover of the Pennines. Hen Cloud is one of the dramatic hills and crags they call 'The Roaches'. They saw-tooth up out of the land body, darkly silhouetted against the skyline, like exposed vertebrae.

This is just beyond the very southern extent of Northumbria, as the ancient Kingdom swung to the west, towards Merseyside, via the Forest of Bowland. But somehow, this landscape belongs in the North. It is reminiscent of the Northumbrian Great Whin Sill and Sandstone Hills, the rougher edges of Yorkshire moors and, in some ways, it is even more dramatic.

My spirits lift as I plough on along a path overgrown to the sides with self-seeded birch and staunch sticks of broom, in bright yellow flower. Carpets of bilberry (or maybe cloudberry) and heather lie between.

Then, most exciting of all, I begin to notice 'clouds', not of hens, but butterflies, each no bigger than a penny. They are the uncommon green hairstreak and I have never encountered so many at once, a 'parade' of hairstreaks, all glistening in their emerald, sun-glancing iridescence. They appear to be gorging themselves, if you can gorge so delicately, on the broom.

It is another one of those moments experienced quite often in the hills, tiny detailed lives being lived out in microcosm, against the backdrop of an infinitely bigger picture.

Reaching the shoulder of the craggy summit, I am confronted by an orange line of emergency fencing and a simple sign, 'caution birds nesting'. I can guess at what it is about and my thoughts are confirmed immediately by the indiscreet, screeching calls of newly fledged peregrine falcons, evidently in residence, somewhere below.

I settle into a cosy hollow in the spring sun and gaze upwards. Just then, two peregrines fly over, jabbing at each other with outstretched talons, working up to a full grapple. Their calls reverberate off the rocks and if I close my eyes, they could be young eagles in the skies of Dakota.

I sit up and take in the view from the Hen Cloud, over The Roaches. Below and to the right there are five smaller crags in a neat row, the so called 'Five Clouds', which look like block-heads, rising from the green shoulders of turf, in which they are buried. Other formations appear vertical and faceted, like Easter Island statues, some almost sphinx shaped. Farther off, there are tors of boulders, resembling cairns made by giants. Later I pass the 'winking man' a massive, wind-sculpted boulder on its natural plinth, shaped into a Mr Punch-like, scowling face; its rock slit eye seems to open and close again as I angle past.

The undulating hills contrast dramatically with the dark exposures of ice-shattered grits. There's something foreboding about the crags' uncompromising sharpness, the way they hold the shadows around them. It is a land of myth and magic, inviting supernatural interpretation.

Across the moor from Hen Cloud this feeling comes to a point, or more an incision; for in this one place, the landscape appears to turn itself inside out.

Striking off the moor top, I drop into a wooded valley, follow a convoluted path through oak wood, where I can hear a rumbling stream, below. There are small quarries here and there, excerpts of rocks, buried now just below the thin skin of the land. I am approaching 'Lud's Church'.

This is not like any church you might imagine. Its doorway is a split between rock faces, heavily vegetated in fern, bracken and tree roots. A serpentine path takes you in and down into a chasm, the roof of the church is a network, high above, of interlocking branches; its walls are the rocks of The Roaches up close, covered in moss, lichen, ferns and other plants, that can tolerate the gloom. The path weaves between boulders and rock faces, tree roots bind around them, clinging and leaning in places, elbowing out at you. This is a church within the land itself, a deep soul slice into Earth.

'Lud' was the name of the Celtic sun god. It is also known as 'the green chapel' and has been the site of ritual and worship over centuries, even occasionally, today.

On this Northumbrian journey, the importance of Nature, exhibited by the wandering monks of the Celtic church, has been evident from north to south. The monasteries they established at Lindisfarne and throughout the Kingdom, were in liminal places, wild and untamed, where they could feel alive and spiritually uplifted.

Lud's Church is of the same ilk and, like the other Celtic Christian sites, also harks back to earlier Pagan beliefs and sacred practice, venerating Nature. All of these traditions held open air worship, before there were any churches, recognising the special feel of certain locations. Lud's Church is one such and retains something of its intrinsic value, in connecting people to their cosmos. It holds the spirit of the landscape in its sylvan, rock walls.

Rather than threatening, despite the underground sensation, there is a feeling of going into the Earth, being enveloped and perhaps nurtured by it. It reminds me of taking time out from a moorland bike ride, sitting quietly in Lastingham Church crypt: meditating midstream, at the Bronte Waterfall: the atmosphere of Roughting Linn falls: the Hermit's Cell on Iona.

In all these places, I was being held gently by the land itself. I could imagine too, in the days of wildwood England, thousands of years ago, this was the sort of place people sought and used for refuge and ritual. You could sense it had always been so.

But it also holds other, poetic, associations. It is thought to be the place, in Arthurian legend, where Sir Gawain, the youngest around King Arthur's Round Table, met and fought the Green Knight, a monstrous creature, intent on beheading him. The greatest and oldest, surviving, Saxon Nature poem, with all its ancient, mythological connotations, focused in this spot. You might imagine such happenings here, long ago, as you can picture gatherings of people crowding this chasm to immerse themselves, body and soul in Nature over millennia.

I walk up and through the long, steepening ravine and as I do so, the sun splits the clouds and beams of light shine down through the canopy, evaporating the cool dankness and filling the space with yellow-green light. It is as if the sun is shining through an enormous, stained glass roof. Looking around me, history and interpretations, the myths of Man, also disappear into thin air and I stand again in a simple, pure, beautiful space.

Stripped of its stories, it is just a wonderful place to be in the evening light. It feels special and life enhancing. I feel truly alive and connected to all that could be.

I guess that is how it all started for us humans, some moment way back in our evolution, when we realised, for the first time, that some places in Nature are intrinsically special, that make us feel deeply connected, for which we developed a sense of reverence.

I had come a long way south in Northumbria and had inklings of these experiences many times along the way. But somehow, in the green chapel, more than anywhere, I felt at one with the wholeness of Nature and all existence.

*(Lastingham Church crypt, 4-30pm,*
*5th September 2014)*

## *Postscript*

You could say I said a prayer here, meditated; I did both and I made a wish too, as I placed a smooth, round, white Iona pebble, flecked with serpentine, in the window behind the altar above St Chad's tomb.

In the peace and stillness of this sacred place, located between hill and moor I felt that I had travelled to the corners of Northumbria and had brought all of it together, in the here and now.

I had found my 'Way'. All the famed and nameless seekers, who had also sought and found natural energy and spirit of place, across this land before me, would have expected no more and no less.

## Selected Further Reading

The following have provided helpful insights and some of the writings that informed and inspired me along the way.
Simon Armitage, various writings but especially,
The Stanza Stones (Enitharmon Press, 2013) and Walking Home (Faber and Faber, 2012).
Myrtle and Phillip Ashmole, The Carrifran Wildwood Story (Borders Forest Trust, 2009).
William Atkins,The Moor (Faber and Faber, 2014).
Stan Beckensall, Northumberland the Power of Place, Tempus 2001 and Prehistoric Rock Art in Norhumberland, 2006.
Stewart Bonney, editor, The Northumbrian magazine, back issues and Wild Northumberland, Powdene Publicity, 2012.
Ian Dewhirst,The Haworth Water Witch and other Yorkshire Stories (Ridings Publishing, 1967).
Arthur and Doris Holmes, Principles of Physical Geology, (Thomas Nelson and Sons,1978 edition).
Clive King, Stig of the Dump (Puffin, 1963).
Olivia Laing, To the River, Canongate,2012.
Angus Lunn, Northumberland, New Naturalist (Collins, 2004).
Robert Macfarlane, everything but especially, The Old Ways (Penguin, 2012).
Richard Mabey, everything but especially Nature Cure (Chatto and Windus, 2005).
Andrew Meirlon Jones et al An Animate Landscape, Rock Art and the Prehistory of Kilmartin (Windgather Press, 2011).

John Miles, Hadrian's Birds (Jockey Shield, 1992).
Ron Shaw and Roger Smith, Saint Cuthbert's Way Official Guide (Birlinn, 2009).
Brian A. Smith and Alan A. Walker, Rock Art and Ritual in the North York Moors, Tempus, 2008 and Mindscapes of Prehistory (Amberley, 2011).
Frank S. Smythe, The Spirit of the Hills, and other books (Hodder and Stoughton, 1938).
Jenny Uglow, Nature's Engraver (Faber and Faber. 2006).
Clive Waddington, Rescued From The Sea (Archaeological Research Services Ltd, 2014)
Simon Warner, Ways to the Stone House (Bronte Society, 2012).

# *Acknowledgement and Thanks*

I have been writing this book and journeying through Northumbria with intent for over four years, being influenced and inspired along the way by many places, people and writers. For much of this time I suffered with broken hips but walked and explored anyway. Their replacement gave me the ability and zest to complete this journey. I owe a lot to surgeon Andrew Port and his team at James Cook Hospital.

Three influences stand out: the writings of Simon Armitage and the Stanza Stone project, its linkage of landscape and words: discovering the inspiring works of Frank S Smythe, a mountaineer in the 1930s, whose poetic understanding of high places should be more widely appreciated and I rediscovered the magic of the Brontes and their moors.

Thanks to Kim Woolhead for her technical help and support and to Pauline Hughes Plummer for her unfailing positive criticism and editorship and Sheila Wakefield, Founder Editor of Red Squirrel Press for publishing it.

Thanks also to Angus and Jean Lunn and Ian and Pat Armstrong, for their knowledge and inspiration: Chris and Mary Pratt for their support and companionship: Brian A. Smith for sharing theories and evidence on prehistory: Clive Waddington for his archaeological and human perspective: also to archaeologist Steve Sherlock for all that is Street House: Jane and Steve Speak for their directions and Steve's great insights: Conrad and Hilary Dickinson for inspiration; Jean Wiggins, local historian: the Lee Family Redcar team: Gloria, Peggy,

Jason of the Light Foundation: Rocky the birder: Graham, the Whitby fish and fossil finder: JP and Mary Wills for snippets and support: Barry Mead for his whale tales: David Jones for information on old ways through Cheviot: Martin Kitching of Northern Experience for black grouse tips: to Susie White for her bat experiences: Jules for Forest memories. All at NWT who shared their knowledge, help and expertise: similarly John and Rob at YWT and Carlo at LWT. Eileen and Gary for being supportive friends. Apologies for anyone I have missed.

Thanks also to all the great pit stops I found along the way for their rest and refreshment including: the Border Hotel, Kirk Yetholm: The Townhouse, Melrose: Bari Tea Alnwick: Wit's End and Sandside cafes, Sandsend: and the brilliant Becketts of Whitby, still my favourite writing and thinking place: the Runcible Spoon, Hinderwell: Jason and Sue at the Fox and Hounds, Goldsborough: the Old White Lion, Haworth: Old Bewick Farmhouse: 'the Welly', Goole.

Finally thank you to Ratchel, my wife, for her fortitude and confidence in me and staying awake during midnight readings, mostly.

A special mention for **Northumberland Wildlife Trust (NWT) and the Wildlife Trust movement**. Working with everyone at NWT and its consultancy EcoNorth in the cause of conservation is a constant privilege and motivating force. We are helping to shape and conserve the land and wildlife of the north. Working in Northumberland especially, makes you want to delve deeper into its past and understand its living landscapes.

The other northern Trusts, Durham, Tees Valley, Yorkshire, Cheshire, Cumbria, Derbyshire Staffordshire, Sheffield and Lancashire, collectively, as part of the 47 county Trusts, are ensuring wildlife thrives into the future for everyone's benefit. Anyone who loves Northumbria should **join their local Trust** and through their reserves and projects and events, you too will see and experience the amazing biodiversity of the north lands and help save it for future generations. Go to www.nwt.org to join up.